How to Kill Your Husband's Ex, Attorneys and Then Some

Ass Kickin' Advice for Stepmoms

Kathy Hammond

Chelsea → It was great fun getting to know you.

Kathy

Copyright © 2019 Kathy Hammond.

All rights reserved. No part of this book may be reproduced, stored, or transmitted by any means—whether auditory, graphic, mechanical, or electronic—without written permission of both publisher and author, except in the case of brief excerpts used in critical articles and reviews. Unauthorized reproduction of any part of this work is illegal and is punishable by law.

ISBN: 978-1-0824-6380-8

Contents

Chapter 1	Money, Money, Money	1
Chapter 2	Legal Stuff That Can Screw You Up Beyond Your Imagination	11
Chapter 3	Kill All the Lawyers	28
Chapter 4	In-laws and Other "Family"	40
Chapter 5	Disciplining the Kiddies: Who's in Charge Here?	45
Chapter 6	When the Kids Come a Callin'	49
Chapter 7	When Stepkids Misbehave	60
Chapter 8	Dad's Relationship with the Kids	67
Chapter 9	Inheritance: To Give or Not to Give. That is the Question.	75
Chapter 10	The Ex	84
Chapter 11	More Really Important but Miscellaneous Challenges That Didn't Earn Their Own Chapter	90

My Final Thoughts (And I'm Worn Out) 99

To my love, my life and, dare I leave out, catalyst for this book, my husband, John. Without you, this book would not have been possible … or, it may have been possible, but just differently inspired by another cast of characters.

I also dedicate this book to the multitude of stepmoms who enter into marriage to a man with children, and with all good intentions, who may not receive appreciation as they should, for the hard work, sacrifices and frustrations endured that many stepfamilies demand. Without your dedication to making things work and keeping the peace for another's family, society may be worse off. So, while your efforts may be unsung by the lives you impact, know that your influence is far reaching.

Kill [kil]: v., to neutralize

You didn't *really* believe I meant something else, did you?

I wouldn't dream of it. Even twenty-seven years ago after marrying a father of two very young sons. Perhaps I was happily delusional in those early days, especially when, as a wedding gift, a friend gave me a book on stepmotherhood. Choked with tips on what a new stepmom could do to bond with stepkids, I believed everything was going to be just fine.

2.5+ decades later, I now see the book did a supremely lousy job of alerting women to what it really means to be a stepmom.

Not a single word in those pages about unruly stepkids, vindictive ex-wives, the 1,001 ways lawyers can screw you out of your life savings, or what to do when a family so coddles stepkids they are unable to function in adulthood, and, in some instances, blaming stepmom for all the family chaos. Nope. The book oozed sweetness with its guidance on how *stepmom* should tiptoe around every dysfunctional asshole in the stepkid's family lest we traumatize the kiddies further.

Forget the kids may have experienced parents' daily combat, infidelity, drug or alcohol abuse, or other selfish choices parents use to destroy kids' lives. According to this book, the fix for making the stepchildren's lives better was for *stepmom* to create some parallel universe, one where parents hadn't trashed their little lives. And, if stepmom is unable to correct all the wrongs, let's just blame her for all the pain.

Why? you ask. Why not? Do you think parents who have no qualms about destroying their kid's lives so they can trade up to someone or something better or for any other personal reason will assume responsibility for causing their kid pain? Not likely. Under these conditions, I guarantee there is not much insight going on.

I'll betchya' that in the time leading up to **_you_** becoming stepmom, none of this was even a blip on your radar. While fussing over the details of your wedding, you probably don't even see those plotting against you the moment you tie the knot. You likely don't have an inkling that some are betting against the success of your marriage and are feeling pretty confident it won't survive because: 1) Statistics and 2) The aforementioned plot to destroy your marriage. I can tell you, however, how to combat *this* was not in that little book I read oh so long ago.

You're probably thinking, *She's crazy. Life with my fiancé* (or husband if you picked up this book too late) *is better than fantastic. It's heaven. The kids and I are besties and they love our new family. And their mom? She could not be kinder to me. She is so helpful, giving me tips on how to manage those darling hellions. Angry, bitter ex-wives don't behave that way. And my in-laws? I will be their new daughter. This Kathy chick is nuts. Nothing could possibly change this nirvana. We will all live happily ever after.*

Now is not the time to be naïve, dear girl. Forever is a long time.

In the now 27 years I've been a stepmom, I've learned quite a bit about human behavior and the dynamics of a stepfamily. Popularized by Malcolm Gladwell's *Outliers* is the 10,000-hour rule where the author contends it takes approximately ten thousand hours of practice to achieve mastery in a field. While I am certainly not the foremost expert on stepmotherhood, if such a person even exits, given I have invested about 237,000 hours in this role, there might be a thing or two you can glean from my experience.

In the pages that follow, I will share with you the dastardly deeds you would never imagine people would commit against anyone, much less you. Think, however, that blindsiding only happens when caught off-guard. This is *exactly* why I wrote this book. You'll not be blindsided ever or again.

Now, I wish I could tell you that once everyone gets used to the idea of *you*, it will be smooth sailing going forward. Perhaps for some, that is true, and at times, even I thought I had permanently emerged from the rapids. But, big sigh here, unfortunately, I have yet to meet a stepparent who, once having traversed the gauntlet, experienced unending paradise with their stepfamily. However, that doesn't mean it isn't possible. After all, I haven't yet seen the Pyramids of Egypt but I believe they exist.

Be cautioned, however, that to keep your marriage strong, at times you may need to invoke the spirits of saints. You may need to smile through clenched teeth, no matter how shitty and underhanded people behave toward you, show respect to people who don't deserve any, be sly when the situation warrants cunning, and to help your partner gain or maintain a backbone in the face of all that is now or about to be coming your way.

It is a lot of work. I grant you that but, without sounding too cliché, there can be some great rewards, fleeting though they may be. You will most certainly enter into this union believing you can grow a happy and contented family from the carcass of a family left by your husband and his ex. It's an admirable ambition but if you are unsuccessful, please don't blame yourself. Their family was DOA when you showed up.

Statistics shout that second or more marriages don't have much chance of survival. There's a reason for this. It is the principle of time and pressure. Given enough time and pressure, something is bound to break. Competing agendas from many others – an ex, in-laws, the ex's family and friends – in your marriage can put a lot of pressure on two souls. And, if you don't know where to cement the cracks to stop the break lines, the whole thing can come crashing down on your head. But you're in luck. In the past 2.5+ decades, I have learned where and how to seal the fracture lines.

If this book can shorten your learning curve so you can retain power over your life (it is your life, too, after all, regardless of what others believe), I will have done what I set out to do. This may not be all-inclusive, but my hope is that after you read this book, you will be confident in your choices, can effectively help your spouse through trying situations, keep a boatload of money in your pocket, and create a wonderful marriage. If you can develop great relationships with stepkids and in-laws in the process, consider that a MEGA bonus. If you can't, there ain't much you can do as they were broken when you found them.

Welcome to stepmotherhood! Now, go get 'em, tiger.

CHAPTER ONE
Money, Money, Money

For the uninitiated, you may wonder why I chose money as the first topic of discussion and not something like *relationships*. Dear girl, you have much to learn as few things in the post-divorce/stepfamily dynamic riles emotions more than money. Believe me when I tell you this isn't the *Three Bears*, where child support or alimony is ever "just right." No way. Know that for battling duos, nothing is ever "just right."

You may discover that a child support award found to be fair at the time of the divorce now enrages the ex when your husband gains a second income, especially if her financial position remains the same. If money is tight for the ex, she's struggling to uphold her former life, and you and your husband are better off, this could be the trifecta that prompts a vendetta. In situations where post-divorce acrimony is the theme, know this – any involvement by you will surely exacerbate whatever emotions the ex is experiencing about your husband's money.

You could have a lucrative career and even earn more than your husband and the ex still accuses you of squandering your *husband's* money on Prada handbags while claiming their children wear rags. The ex may act out by frustrating custody exchanges or doing something nutty like cancelling the children's health insurance of which your husband pays his ex to cover this expense. She may tell you she is angry because she had trouble paying her electric bill (despite a brand-new car in the garage) while your husband did something (she deems) frivolous with his money.

That you earn your own keep, and then some, won't make you any less of her target.

Yep, money is enough of a sore subject when the only people involved are the divorced parents and their attorneys. Throw a stepmom into the mix and it may resemble wild dogs fighting over a single kill (your husband's income).

I have learned, however, that most money issues in these circumstances are rarely about money. For those who have not yet attained career success or remarried well, reconciled their emotions from the divorce, are immature, or are just being an asshole, money can be the tool to punish or control a former spouse. In the wake of a divorce, the ex may realize that freedom from an unhappy marriage has a substantial price tag – by way of a 50-80% reduction in household income. If unable to make up the difference on her own, she may see taking her ex back to court for more money as a solution to budget misjudgments. And, as you will see in a later chapter, the legal system is the *ideal* vehicle for granting an ex's frequent income raise – even if your husband does not receive one (in which case, you may want to make sure the ex doesn't get her hands on this book, I write, tongue in cheek).

Conversely, when the ex flagrantly disregards the court's orders, your husband may invoke the power of deduction, and not in the logical sense, to force the ex into complying with those orders. This power involves deducting monies from child support until the ex complies with the court's order or drags your husband's ass back into court for *his* violating the court's orders for non-payment of child support. For instance, let's say the ex has a bug up her ass about something and sends the kids to dad for his custody time with a suitcase full of oversized, stained and ragged clothing. Instead of dad calling the ex and asking that she knock it off, as that would not have any effect on someone who would do this in the first place, dad buys new clothes for the kids. Later, at child support time, the receipt for new clothes accompanies a reduced child support check. It works. The ex stops sending crap clothing with the kids for dad's visitation. But wait!

While it may appear to be a power move, it is not. In reality, it is an extremely shortsighted fix. All dad has accomplished is pissing off the ex and motivating her to find other ways to crawl under his and your skin; not to mention, chronicling these instances for a future court appearance, where she sues for *all* of dad's deductions, large and small. An angry ex may not be able to find her shoes under piles of clothes and other junk in her house but make no mistake, lurking under toys, garbage, clothing, blankets and crushed cereal covering floors and kitchen counters, is a meticulously maintained file system containing every receipt and scrap of paper given to her by your husband since the moment the ink started drying on the very first child support order.

My aim here is not to provide you with power moves to get even with or control the ex. Good gracious, dear. Life is too freakin' short to spend it plotting against someone who is clearly struggling with stuff that has zero to do with you or your husband (unless, of course, your husband did something naughty to get out of the marriage). No. My goal is to keep *you* sane, content and with a lot of moolah in your pocket.

For all you know, the havoc the ex wreaks in your lives may be because she realizes she trashed her marriage and family, believing her life would instantly become better, post-divorce. If things did not turn out as she hoped, you and your husband may just be her punching bag. This is definitely not someone you want to engage in warfare. The more you can do to remove yourselves from the ex's line of sight, the happier you and your husband will be.

This means there are things you and your husband can do to lessen the angst. I caution you that many of these solutions require a certain level of maturity on the part of your husband, his ex and you for these to work. Naturally, you do not possess the ability to make people grow up or to stop causing problems, but it is within your power to control yourself. Nevertheless, the following tips are certainly worth taking a shot to eliminate many money-related disputes.

So, let's begin with …

Only your husband is to send child support checks to his ex.

For some, the courts make a wage assignment for child support payments that the dreaded Child Support Services processes. For others, one parent pays the other. If child support services deducts child support from his paycheck, you can move onto the next tip. If, however, your husband makes payments directly to the ex, pay very close attention.

There is probably nothing more irritating to a disgruntled ex than seeing your elegant signature – bearing the same last name, no less! – on a child support check as it serves as a monthly reminder of your existence – something the ex likely tries to forget. It can also represent another woman's power over *her* finances as you dole out her monthly "allowance." And come on, we know why you were only too happy to take on this task. Tsk. Tsk. If I were on the receiving end of a new wife sending me money for the support of children I made with my ex, my thoughts might not be so benevolent. Know this, though: When mama is annoyed, others are soon to follow.

When I first married, I rationalized that because I like managing my finances, I should be in charge of sending support payments, as child support was just another financial obligation. Trust me. It's not the same as an electric bill.

So, here's my first big piece of advice to you: **Have your husband handle it.** Your husband is a grown-up, or should be, and he can write a few numbers on a piece of paper and mail it without your assistance. If he can't, well, dear girl, his ex dodged the bullet but you did not.

If you feel you simply must maintain control, pay online. This makes paying child support effortless and blameless. It may be handy to know, however, that banks retain records for only seven years yet there is no statute of limitations in most states on the collection of unpaid child support. As banks no longer return cancelled checks in the mail and records are kept for only seven years, stay tuned, as this can affect your future.

Additionally, there are other reasons you will read about where having your husband handle this obligation can add years to your life and marriage.

If your husband complains about paying child support, ask him to (*please, dear God*) stop.

Your husband knew or should have known the stakes when he had children so if he's lousy at choosing women (say what?) or was a lousy husband and the ex wanted out, well, those were his choices. As such, there are consequences for his choices, including supporting children he made and he needs to take his as a man.

Would he prefer the kid go hungry? Is it the ideal situation? Absolutely not. Can you argue the kid could live with you, eliminating the need for child support altogether, at least from your husband to his ex? Of course you could but that is not likely to happen. So, if the kid's living arrangement isn't going to change, what's the point of expending energy railing against a stonewall? Gently remind your husband of his responsibilities whenever the complaints start coming. After that, ignore his complaints.

I need to add that I used to think because I chose my husband, whatever pain he endured from those choices was also my cross to bear. To a certain extent, OK, considering the whole 'two becomes one' premise of marriage. Still, no use both of us feeling crummy. Allow him to deal with his own shit. He has children to support. Too bad if the ex is making his life hell in the wake of the split up. He picked her.

Do not (directly, if you can't contain yourself) accuse the mother of squandering child support monies on herself.

You never see the ex in the same outfit twice. Her shoe buying rivals Imelda Marcos (history lesson, girl). She is well massaged, coifed, travels, and buys a new car every three years while she purchases the kid's wardrobe from church bazaars, all the while your husband doles out thousands of dollars in support. My advice: Get over it.

What's that you say?

You're probably thinking you made the worst investment with this book – especially when your husband's ex owns more Jimmy Choo's than Jimmy himself and whose lipstick collection single-handedly put Sephora on the map. Just hear me out. I'm not as crazy as you might think.

Consider that, in many cases, the ex works full-time. That means whatever she does with her money is none of your business. Unless the kids are in honest-to-goodness rags and without shoes, while their mother's best friends are Louis Vuitton and Christian Dior, how she spends her money and that of child support is entirely her affair. If not Blue Ivy or a Kardashian, know that many parents don't shell out big bucks, nor should they, for kids' clothes because kids outgrow clothes and/or destroy them. The pricey sweater I bought my seven-year-old nephew for his birthday lasted only one day after he left it on the school playground, never to be seen again. And some kids, especially the younger ones, don't care about clothes. But most importantly, a kids' generic-label or ill-fitting wardrobe is simply not worth getting worked up about. Good grief, people. There are people starving in the world. Who really gives a shit about the three sizes too large sweatpants on your three-year-old stepson?

Besides, if a mother doesn't care how her kids look, why should you? I know, you're thinking, *When they are with me, people think they are my kids.* Well, I have a couple of great answers for this: 1) If it bothers you so much, keep clothes you prefer at your house and 2) People who know you and the kids, know they aren't your kids and people who don't know you, who cares what they think? You won't see them again. Don't you have better things to worry about? This book is about preserving your mental well-being.

But I am also not a complete Polly Anna; not anymore, at least. I realize some exs intend to give the appearance of living the high life while the kid looks like a waif. Some moms purposely pack the absolute worst clothing the kids have, clothes so food-and-ink stained they appear tie-dyed for their weekly visit to dad. There are all kinds of tricks moms use to stir the pot to get you and your husband's juices flowing. If this happens to you, refer to what I said earlier – it's not worth getting worked up about. Besides, if you do get upset, and that was the mother's goal, you will only fuel her fire to do more. As Byron Katie penned: "Defense is the first act of war."

Think about that.

And let's not forget one very important point: If statistics bear out, there is an even greater chance of *you* becoming an ex than there was for the first one. How would you feel about the next wife scrutinizing *your* spending?

Keep a separate bank account from your husband.

I am not a fan of separate bank accounts in a marriage. If you also believe in joint accounts, be prepared to divulge *your* personal financial information to the ex for every child support/alimony issue that lands up in court. Your husband will have to cough up his financial information and if you have co-mingled funds in an account, the ex will absolutely know how much you earn, what you spend on manicures and massages, if you are hiding a boat, and how well you are doing with your investments.

However, if you have no concerns about others knowing your financial business or are doing exceedingly well and want to rub the ex's face in it, then, by all means, maintain joint accounts. If your joint investments are sizable enough, you may want to prepare for your husband to make more court appearances in the future, if for no other reason than to see if any more money can be wrangled from him. Of course, there may be ways around having your portion of the proceeds exempted from any court orders, but, considering what lawyers charge (and there is a whole lot more discussion in this book on this subject) to sort out these situations, you're better off just keeping your information to yourself.

So, if not wanting to flame the fires, you may also want to consider choosing a different filing status for income tax returns if you are really hell bent on the ex not knowing what you earn. Disclaimer: I am not a tax expert and this is only my personal opinion. I am merely pointing out ways in which the ex can learn about your personal finances and how you can keep this from happening.

Prohibit your husband from listing your personal property as marital property on income and expense statements in child support cases.

I know, philosophically, after you marry, 'what's mine is yours' but if ex hauls your husband back into court, "yours" may become "hers" if your husband lists your property in court documents as marital property and a court entitles the ex to attach those assets. That Picasso you picked up for a song? While it may hang in the living room you and hubby share, if your husband lists it as an asset, there may be some wrestling to be had.

I collect art, before and after I married. My husband and I also bought a house for my elderly mother with dementia and retained title in both of our names. When my husband sought a change in custody after one of his sons lived with us for a few years, the ex countered with an expected (because, hey, why not? You're going to court anyway) countersuit for unpaid child support. As required by the courts, my husband listed all assets we owned together *and* separately as *marital* property on the Income and Expense statement. This included the art I bought before we married and, as we should have, the house we bought for my mother. The ex and her attorney zeroed in on those items as possible assets – for the ex, should the Court find in her favor. (Fortunately, the Court got most of it right that time so no jeopardy to my property.)

While I don't encourage dishonesty, property acquired before you married is not legally your husband's property. In fact, if you were to divorce, you most likely would get to keep that property. If your husband omits your property from an income and expense statement, he isn't being deceitful. Stuff you acquire after you marry, especially property recorded in government records, well, that's a different story.

Recommend to your husband that he meet with his ex on an annual basis to review the kid's financial needs.

If money is an issue between your husband and the ex, you will undoubtedly think I am crazy suggesting he give her even more money. However, this one tip, alone, provided the ex goes along with it, has the potential to save you and your family enough money to buy a new car or vacation home. I jest not. Read on!

Despite what a lawyer might tell you, it is not mandatory that *every* money discussion between your husband and his ex also happen with attorneys or in front of a judge. Attorneys only want you to think it does so you will continue to invite them into your wallet. From personal experience, legal fees can choke the life out of you when your husband and his ex wage even the smallest of battles. The ex is tired of telling little Billy he can't have new Nikes. Solution: Sue dad. When emotions run high, as they typically do in family law, a court fight is the equivalent of giving an attorney a blank check.

First, the ex throws a blow, your husband returns it, then she, then he … the fight is on, emotions are raw, each trying to get the better of the other. Meanwhile, back at their offices, the attorneys puff on fat cigars, counting stacks of your and the ex's money and perusing yacht listings all because the ex is trying to sneak in a couple of extra weeks of custody on her ledger so your husband will have to pay an additional 50 bucks a month in child support and your husband is going to fight to the death to prevent it. While the attorneys dream about a 65' Marquis cruiser with cherry wood accented staterooms, your husband contributes to their yacht fund as he fights against a $600/year increase.

Picture me shaking my head. Ridiculous, right? And yet every day, thousands of couples buy their attorneys new cars and put their kids through college. If the attorneys are really lucky and they get themselves a couple of lunatics who can't or won't put on the brakes with the fighting, we're talking house buying!

Is this truly how you and your husband want to spend your time and money?

However, repeat court appearances happen when the ex feels your husband can be doing (read: paying) so much more, the kid's needs change, or the ex is having a difficult time keeping up financially. Like irascible tectonic plates, something's going to give, and in a very big way, when applying enough pressure. The fix can be simple. Relieve the pressure along the way to avoid a catastrophe.

Your husband meeting with his ex, in the spirit of cooperation versus combat, allows both parties to *calmly* discuss how best to take care of their kid's needs. And as anyone with kids will tell you, their needs increase with age so it best to accept and plan for it. If you receive pushback from your spouse, remind him that had his family remained intact, he would have been having these money discussions with his former partner and finding a solution. Ask your husband to remind his ex of the same if she is reluctant to cooperate. She may agree. If not, you are in no worse a position than before asking.

It may actually occur that in anticipation of a kid's desire (or mom's wish for the kid) to participate in a costly activity, the ex will accept a one-time payment rather than seek court assistance for more child support, which could result in a monthly increase over the *lifetime* of the support order. Consider that a $100 per month increase in child support over ten years ($12,000) plus attorney fees, is a more bitter pill to swallow than paying the ex $1,000 now so the kid can go to camp.

This is not foolproof as there are some exs who delight in being unreasonable and making others suffer. This is also not insurance to guard against the ex accepting the additional money from your husband and later suing him for an increase in support. Anything can happen and no one can control another. However, if the ex is a reasonable person who may occasionally struggle financially or the kid needs something, this one tip alone has the potential of saving you and your family major bucks, not to mention eliminating the anxiety of battling it out in court.

CHAPTER TWO

Legal Stuff That Can Screw You Up Beyond Your Imagination

And you thought all those legal documents between your husband and his ex would have nothing to do with you. OK, sure.

I once thought the same. It didn't occur to me that my then-fiancé's custody and child support orders would ever affect *my* life, at least not to any major extent. Those were agreements previously worked out between my fiancé, his ex, and their attorneys, a nice tidy package both parties would unfailingly adhere to for the duration of the agreement. Naturally, we would need to accommodate visitation schedules and, of course, there were child support and other financial obligations but, from what my fiancé told me in the beginning, it all seemed quite ... trivial.

Ah, blissful ignorance.

For starters, it turned out things weren't quite as buttoned up as my fiancé portrayed. Not long after we married, I learned my husband was in the throes of an unresolved lawsuit his ex had filed for an increase in child support and contempt for unpaid child support, while my husband had counter-sued for the ex's failure to pay an expense mandated by the original divorce settlement. For some unknown reason, the lawsuit stalled but reared its ugly little head not long after our nuptials. Yes, that can happen.

As the ex had filed the lawsuit only six months after finalizing their divorce, and my husband hearing legal horror stories from others in post-divorce war, he believed post-divorce lawsuits were *normal*; so much so that he didn't think it important to tell me. Unless you are an attorney, know that lawsuits are not normal. However, for my husband and his ex, this was their way of *communicating*. Can you believe it?

For example, let's say an ex-wife demands that her ex-husband keep the kids for a few extra days beyond his scheduled weekend custody so she may vacation with her boyfriend. However, the ex-husband can't accommodate *extra* days as he will be out of town on business. Rather than the ex rescheduling her vacation and adhering to the court order, she steals the kids out of daycare and to her parents, in another state, before her ex-husband can pick the kids up for his scheduled weekend visitation. When the ex-husband learns the ex absconded with the kids to her parents, he calls his former in-laws to tell them he's coming to get the kids. So, let's also say the ex's parents announce to their former son-in-law that they have, somehow, miraculously, without a court hearing, and in the two hours it took their daughter to drive the kids to their house, obtained a *restraining order* against him, and threaten him with arrest if he attempts to get his kids for his court-ordered visitation. Hmmm. That's a tough one.

The ex-husband has a few options: 1) Drive hundreds of miles to the former in-laws, where there may be a scene in getting the kids and, potentially, traumatizing them, 2) Attempt to get the police involved to help him retrieve his kids, again, potentially traumatizing them (or, as it happens, having the police tell him it's a civil matter to be handled by the courts), 3) Call the ex and berate her, having little to no effect while she sips Piña Coladas on a beach, 4) File a motion for contempt with the court for her violating visitation, begging expensive and time draining court appearances and still not getting the kids or 5) Do nothing. Not a single attractive option. The issues propelling people into court are life sucking enough as they are; even more excruciating when draining your savings to discuss this crap in court, none of which will ever replace the time lost between dad and kids.

So, what to do?

No matter how wronged your husband is or may feel, try all other available means to resolve whatever issue arises; unless, of course, the ex is habitually denying access to or is harming a kid (more on this later). And by 'harm', I don't mean the ex sends the kid to school with hot dogs every day or their underwear has other children's names emblazoned on the waistbands. That may be unhealthy or cheap, but it doesn't amount to child endangerment or the ex purposefully frustrating the court's orders. Save time before judges for something really egregious.

However, for those of you whose husbands are in the middle of a legal proceeding with his ex, the following tips can help reduce your financial and emotional burden. If this information comes too late, perhaps these suggestions will be useful in the future. For others about to embark on a marriage to a man with kids, pay very close attention to the following first three suggestions. They may very well open your eyes to what you may need to live with for a very long time.

And on *my* attorney's advice, allow me to stress again that the tips contained in this book are mere suggestions from the insights I've gleaned from the past quarter-century plus of being a stepmom and should not be construed as legal advice under any circumstances. Geez, we can't ever seem to escape the legal stuff, can we?

Demand to read all court documents your husband has pertaining to child support, custody, visitation, alimony; find out if he is involved in any pending court cases, preferably *before* you marry.

People who make repeat visits to the courthouse to hash out issues over support and visitation sometimes see lawsuits as part of the normal ebb and flow of post-divorce life. In the divorced dads' minds, pending lawsuits, outrageous custody/support arrangements, etc. may not be worthy of discussion before they tie the knot with a subsequent spouse. However, as the subsequent spouse, you are entitled to and should know about *any* legal arrangement your fiancé/husband has that will involve consumption of your time, energy, or money. And if they are part of your husband's life, believe me, they will impact the hell out of yours.

With the majority of second marriages doomed from the start, consider that a shaky marriage may become even more hellish when discovering there are others who now control your finances. Whereas pre-marriage, you called all the shots with your money, there may now be a minimum of four other entities involved in your financial life – 1) your husband, 2) his ex, 3) attorneys, and, 4) courts.

It may come about that because of a few white sheets of paper, staycations now supplant your usual tropical vacations as it is the kid taking to the skies for visits with dad, with dad footing the bill. You may discover that even should your husband lose this job, he still has the court-ordered pleasure of sending his kid to Europe to study for the summer or state laws require your husband simultaneously pay college tuition *and* monthly child support. There can be a whole lot of landmines in those legal documents of his that can curb your lifestyle and life plans. If you're to make the best choices for *your* life, you need all the information that has the ability to impact your life.

And to think they say *only* 67% of second marriages end in divorce. (Perhaps the other 33% are found in murder statistics?)

If nothing else, knowing your fiancé's legal obligations to his children will help you come to terms with what will be your new reality before taking the big leap to make other decisions, if you get my drift.

Post-marriage, demand to review any legal documents your husband is to sign before he signs them.

If you keep your distance from your husband's interactions with his ex, you can be objective should he find himself embroiled in a child support or custody lawsuit. Hanging back allows you to objectively understand what the documents are *really* saying (not as crystal clear as one might believe), absent clouded emotions, especially when reading the ex wants the kid to spend Father's Day with her new boyfriend instead of dad or demanding your husband produce personal financial documents of which the ex is not entitled to see. Little things like that.

But, if you have been in the thick of things with your husband from the start, your clarity ain't gonna be all that much better than his. As the opposing side hopes will happen, you will be seething and frustrated during the hours long struggle to keep the ex and the attorneys out of your wallet. From that struggle comes a clouded head so you or your husband won't even realize when the ex's attorney slips in a little provision requiring your husband buy boats for his kids when they graduate high school. As the ex and her attorney lobs one grenade after another at your husband, you'll be so busy trying to dodge them that the exhaustion will drive you both to agree to just about anything to end the assault and your husband's attorney's hourly bill rate of $375+.

Having grown wiser after each of my husband's legal tussles, in one lawsuit with his ex, and after his ex and my husband came to an agreement, I asked my husband not to sign the agreement until I read it. I figured he was exhausted from the endless haggling and I could be his voice of reason. As fortune would have it – that crazy fortune! – he said he had already signed the agreement. But, he said, joyfully, it was all good and everyone was happy. There was even a lilt to his voice.

Ah, delusion. Or, maybe he was drunk when he signed. Had he and his attorney knocked back a few at lunch? I mean, the only reason you hire an attorney is so when there exists a giant fucking hole in the earth in front of their client, the attorney, who has seen many a giant fucking holes in the earth in front of their clients, will shout, "Hey, [Insert Client Name Here], you are standing on the edge of a giant fucking hole. If you take another step, you'll fall into that giant fucking hole. To get out will cost you three times what it cost you to get into this giant fucking hole. I got you, man. You ain't gonna fall into no giant fucking holes on my watch!"

Not the guy my husband hired.

Here we come, giant fucking hole.

The agreement my husband signed, at his attorney's urging no less, required my husband pay the lion's share of daycare until his kids graduated *college*. Yes, you are reading this correctly. *Daycare through college.* At the time of this agreement, the kids were just 9 and 10 years old. We didn't even know they were in daycare. And I am not even sure daycare was an allowable expense for kids that age. When I was 10, *I* was the babysitter.

To be fair to my husband (screw the attorney), the agreement did not spell it out exactly as such. Instead, the new child support amount included my husband's share of alleged *current* daycare expenses, despite no proof the kids were in daycare – more about stuff like this later – but did not include a termination date for childcare expenses. And in the state where the children then resided, the law requires the non-custodial parent pay child support until a child completes college. See? Giant fucking hole.

To terminate daycare expenses later would absolutely, unequivocally risk the ex filing a countersuit for an increase in support, along with, you guessed it, my husband incurring additional attorney fees. If not taking that route, the child support award remains as is and would stay that way until modified by a Court or … that's right, until the kids graduated college. And don't believe your husband can just deduct childcare or other costs once that expense stops for the mom (provided it ever started, right?) unless the order clearly states he can. Your husband needs a court order to reduce any amount rolled into child support or bad shit can happen.

It's the little things, the way things are worded, intentionally omitted information, or overlooked details that can cause big and/or expensive problems down the road that require objectivity to stop before they begin. You can't help your husband if you are in the trenches with him and he signs documents he just wants to dispense with as quickly as possible, even if he has no idea what he agreed to.

You may also learn that once your husband and his ex reach an agreement, one of the two attorneys will then draft the agreement for both parties to sign. In many instances, the ex's attorney will draft the agreement in such a way that it undermines the agreement they just reached. Shocker, huh? That agreement may appear to reflect the actual agreed upon terms but, upon close inspection, does not. At that point, one or both attorneys may apply pressure on your husband to sign the document, perhaps leading your husband to believe he has no other choice. Some unscrupulous attorneys may go so far as to tell their client they have to sign.

However, that's not the truth. He does have another choice. He can trash the document until it reads exactly as they've agreed. If there's no meeting of the minds, it goes before the judge. It's just time and money, baby.

To illustrate how all this can go down, in another legal scrap between my husband and his ex, after an entire day of back-and-forth with the ex and her attorney, they reached an agreement, with the ex's attorney to draft their agreement in writing. My husband and I had traveled to court in the ex's state and had a return flight the following morning so time wasn't on our side. This time, my husband reviewed the "agreement" in detail and found it did not reflect the agreement they reached. Gee, can you imagine?

So, he refused to sign it. However, it was nearing 5 P.M. and the attorneys wanted to go home. My husband did not budge. (Oh, happy day!)

Rather than returning to the ex's attorney to correct the errors, as his attorney should have, my husband's attorney admonished my *husband* with, "If you don't sign it, then you will need to come back. *Is that what you really want?*"

Sure. Why not just live with a decade's worth of untenable conditions instead of my husband's attorney reminding the ex's attorney what they agreed upon and then correct it? How difficult is that?

But it was quittin' time for the attorneys, so I guess pretty damn difficult. So, the parties left the courthouse, with another date scheduled to resolve the issue. Not three weeks later, the ex announces that she and second husband are divorcing, she had signed a lease on an apartment in another county and enrolled the kids in school (in violation of the law, no less), effectively changing everything she and my husband just spent thousands of dollars fighting over during their last visit to the courthouse.

I can see you are now getting it, you clever little monkey, so here are some tips to help you minimize or avoid, altogether, potential legal issues.

Before an attorney files a lawsuit, files a response to a lawsuit and, most especially, prepares any agreement, examine and question EVERY SINGLE SENTENCE.

With an attorney's many years of education and training, it is tempting to believe that what they write is logical and easily interpretable. So, when an attorney inserts something like this into an agreed order: *The parties agree child support is below federal child support guidelines provided Father continues to deposit $80 per month per child into the children's savings accounts,* it appears straightforward, right?

Let's take a closer look, shall we? First, there is no such thing as "federal" child support guidelines; only state guidelines. A layperson probably doesn't know this. Clearly, neither does the attorney who wrote this.

Second, if the father stops contributing to the savings accounts, does child support increase? If so, to what amount? Does the father have a right to stop contributing to the accounts? I mean, the word "provided" indicates he has a choice. Under what circumstances may dad stop paying? Because he doesn't feel like it anymore? Because his attorney raped his bank account and now he's broke? And how would anyone, including the ex, even know he no longer contributes to the accounts? On that point, does the ex have the right to know about deposits? And the pièce de résistance: What is to happen with all this money? Does dad have to turn over tens of thousands of dollars to, say, a drug addicted or otherwise troubled kid? If dad has to hand over the dough, can the kid spend the cash on a friend's stuffed hot dog start-up? Can they use it to buy a house? Juggling lessons?

The words appear harmless yet can be lethal when subject to various interpretations.

But we're not done. Let's fast forward ten years. The two exs have been mixing it up with court appearances for a decade and each is aching to level the other. Mother whips out what she believes is an ace-in-the-hole: those damn savings accounts. In her lawsuit, or response to dad's lawsuit, she states she has no idea if father has been depositing these monies into the savings accounts. OK, no harm in the chick wondering.

When this matter gets before the judge, mother's attorney raises the issue of the savings accounts. Father is silent, refusing to turn over any documentation to the court to prove deposits into accounts. Why? Because mother's pleading is not a pleading at all. It is a mere ponderance and nothing in the ex's court order(s) gives the mother a right to *audit* the savings accounts. And since the order is completely silent on the purpose or distribution of the money in the accounts, dad ain't got to do nothin', except, and here's the kicker – engage in an expensive court battle to point this out to a judge.

Father's attorney failing to adequately illustrate these points to the judge can kinda', pseudo cause an issue, as in the judge issuing a proclamation that father owes his children (who aren't party to the agreed order – interesting) the money that *should have* (mind you, the ex and the court have no clue what's happening with the money) accumulated in the accounts and then, you've got to love America, states, without any legal justification, the *children,* again, not party to the agreement, have the right to sue their father for the money. Even if the kid makes their living as an arms dealer, I suppose.

All this for one little, completely ambiguous sentence. Way to go judges!

People spend a lot of time and money in courts battling over the meaning of clauses in legal agreements. Each sentence in a contract or other legal agreement must be so crystal clear as to not leave a single question for either party. Your husband may be so used to ever-changing legal agreements that he's now only skimming the documents before laying down his signature. With the aim of this book to eliminate the hiring of lawyers and court appearances, investing the time in getting things right at the start will save you time, energy and money so scrutinize every single, solitary word before any deal is consummated.

Urge (beg, plead with) your husband to refrain from filing a lawsuit if missing a handful of visits with the kids. Instead, keep a calendar.

It is my sincere hope that most mothers do not use their children to get what they want or to punish the father. That said, some mothers do. If you are dealing with the latter, understand your husband will be outraged every time the ex messes with his visitation. Other than going to court to enforce visitation, there really isn't a heck of a lot your husband can do. In fact, most judges won't do a damn thing to the ex if there are only a few visits missed. And if a mother has no compunction denying her children access to their father, should your husband seek the court's support, by way of a lawsuit against the ex, the ex will likely retaliate with a motion to modify – upwards – child support. After all, she'll have to file a response to your husband's lawsuit anyway so why not ask for more dough?

Child support increases, you and your husband incur more legal fees, and, without a way to make up missed visits, what was the point?

Where's the justice? you might ask. Not at the courts, and not for something like this. Perhaps in that rare circumstance a judge slaps mom's hand and may even put a little fear in her if she pulls this stunt again, but I wouldn't play those odds in Vegas.

I have a far better solution: Have your husband (if he won't, you do it) keep a calendar of all court-ordered custody exchanges that are to occur and note if they took place or other circumstances surrounding the visit(s) that do not comply with the court's order. If, for example, the court order says mom is to drop off the kids at 6 PM every other Friday and mom brings the kids after 6 PM, record it. If mom decides that two court ordered holidays in one month is just way too many for her to accommodate, telling your husband he must choose one or the other, write that sucker down. If the ex is a no-show at the meeting point and, after tracking her down after waiting with the kids for an hour at said meeting point and the ex says she just didn't feel like going to the meeting point and dad needs to incur an additional hour drive time to return the kids to the ex – broken record here – write it down. Like a McDonald's Monopoly game, collect enough infractions and your husband just may win – custody of his kid, that is.

It must be a substantial amount of missed or screwed up visits to get notice from a judge as courts deal with more serious issues than your husband missing a visit or two (or even three) with his kids. Certainly, it's not right your husband and his children miss any time together. A parent who does this to their own *kid* just shows how little they really care about the kid, despite their protests to the contrary. Funny how that works, right? However, other children face unimaginable problems, so many judges view contempt motions for a handful of missed visits as petty by comparison. Weirdly, the courts don't see a mother's motion for an increase in support as trivial even if it has only been a few months since her last motion to increase support. Go figure.

If the kid changes hands, ask your husband to file for a change of custody and child support the moment your state no longer considers this a temporary arrangement.

In the state that issued one of many child support and custody orders for my husband's kids, thirty (30) continuous days out of the primary custodial parent's care is called a *de facto* change of custody; meaning, a legal change of custody occurred absent an official order by the Court. While that state also abates (suspends) child support after a *de facto* change of custody, this does not mean the tables automatically turn and the *ex* is now required to pay your husband child support. Without a new court order, the ex is free to do absolutely nothing. Nada. Zip. Blow off the kids. Make 'em beg on street corners for lunch money. Ok, maybe not that far.

Sadly, and in a lot of cases (watch Judge Judy), until a Judge issues an official order, some parents will simply not contribute to their children's care. Some parents who gave up primary custody don't even think to buy their kid a pair of socks but will shamelessly honeymoon in Europe, buy a mini-mansion and hit designer racks with total abandon. I mean, you can buy a lot of Prada if not paying for food, clothing and shelter for the little ones, right?

However, and this is a biggie, if you live in a state where they <u>do not abate child support</u> when the kid changes parental hands, your husband could find himself supporting the children AND paying a large sum of child support arrears to the ex if a court did not modify the child support order. He might even go to jail, have his driver's license revoked, and passport confiscated while he tries to sort it out. Under these circumstances, if your husband does not confirm the law before cutting off the money supply to the ex, you must do it unless you relish the idea of driving your husband everywhere he needs to go, ditching your long-awaited Paris trip and visiting your husband behind steel.

If your husband must go to Court, don't go with him.

I said it before in Chapter One but it bears repeating. Again and again and again. Despite harboring fantasies of watching your husband's attorney shred his ex to pieces on the stand to expose her lies and malfeasance, chances are that will never happen and you'll be even more frustrated when it doesn't. You will then want to lash out at his attorney who doesn't want you there because you don't lend anything to the proceedings (except to help pay their fees) and are probably annoying the hell out of them. Your presence will also frustrate your husband as you will be saying one thing while his attorney will likely be saying something different.

There is absolutely nothing for you to gain in this situation so it is best to just stay away from the court; unless, of course, you are under subpoena as a witness to the proceedings, in which case, you may need to ...

Prepare to be disposed by the ex's attorney for court proceedings.

If the ex is particularly vengeful, or is just not a nice person, she and her attorney may demand you take part in a deposition. This means the ex's attorney gets to ask you lots of questions about everything. Nothing is off-limits.

Typically, the purpose of the ex deposing *you* is simply to hassle you and run up your husband's legal fees as your husband's attorney will attend your deposition. Of course, it will also run up the ex's legal fees, but in a battle, people tend to throw sensibility out the window. And know that your husband's attorney is not there to represent you as they are not *your* attorney, even if your hard-earned money goes to them.

If you find yourself in a deposition, remain calm. The ex's attorney will likely attempt to intimidate you and say you are required to divulge intimate conversations between you and your husband and if you don't, something terrible will happen to you. Yeah, right. What are they gonna' do? Waterboard you?

This is where you can have a little bit of fun. When you meet the ex's attorney insist that you be called *Mrs. (Your Last Name)*, while repeatedly calling the attorney by their first name. Appear aloof, bored or disinterested during the attorney's questions or, better yet, appear perplexed and ask them to rephrase – as many times as you wish. The most that will happen is that people will think you're dumb. Like-a-fox, baby.

If, however, a looming deposition worries you, as you are not sure what information you can withhold and you have some pretty juicy stuff you absolutely don't want to see come to light, check your local court's deposition rules as to what information you can keep to yourself. Just know that unless you've been directly involved in something germane to the proceedings, the intent in deposing you is usually the ex's attempt to screw with you that may leave you saying, "*Screw this. I could be sailing the Greek Isles instead of dealing with this shit,*" and then packing your bags for said Greek Isles. One can certainly dream, baby.

Ignore whatever the ex writes about you in court documents.

You may be offended to read in the ex's court pleadings accusations that you starve the kid or that all you do is sleep and work. You may read that because of *your* work schedule, *your husband* is unable to spend quality time with the kid and for that reason, the court should deny dad custody or additional visitation. In fact, you may read a whole lot of shit about you that is flat-out untrue or are twisted truths, such as the blending of two or three separate events that would make even Mother Teresa appear a monster; the latter, one of the more clever ways to irritate the shit out of someone. I mean, if three unrelated events are standalone truths, such as, 1) Went to a party, 2) Talked with Sam, 3) Embarrassed by what you did, when combining them into a single event, it looks like you went to a party where you talked with Sam and now you are embarrassed by what you did. Ooooh. People are gonna' talk!

I have only one thing to say to this: *Sticks and stones*, so ignore it. It means nothing to a judge unless the ex produces actual evidence that the kid is, in fact, emaciated at your hands or has suffered some other injury. This isn't the first rodeo for many of these judges and they know parents make outrageous claims without anything to back up those claims. And understand that many attorneys *encourage* their clients to make unsubstantiated claims solely to fan the flames and turn what could and should be a simple proceeding into a brawl that (insert gasp here) puts more money in their pockets. Would you believe such a thing?

So, how should your husband respond to these accusations? One word: *Deny.* That's it. One word is all that is required in your husband's responsive pleadings for each accusation leveled by his ex. Unless the ex can prove her allegations, everything stops right there. Seriously. It doesn't go any farther than that as it is up to the *accuser* to prove their allegations. Except, of course, when it applies to child support payments. Your husband would have to prove payments made if the ex accuses him of not paying child support. See the following suggestion for more on this.

Reading the ex's accusations *will* absolutely piss you off. You will want, may even demand, that your husband set the record straight by launching a public relations campaign via his responsive pleadings to demonstrate to the court (the world?) that you really are a good person. DON'T DO

IT! First, a judge doesn't care. Second, it will only increase your husband's legal fees. And *that* will really piss you off.

Should the ex level accusations of you physically abusing the children, this is an entirely different matter and the ex should be set straight by a judge. Your husband's attorney can advise your husband on how this should be handled.

Keep records of all child support/alimony payments.

If an action is brought against your husband for unpaid support of any kind and he can't produce the records, guess what? He gets to pay again. And since banks only keep records for seven years and many states don't have a statute of limitations on collecting child support or alimony, this means it is up to your husband or you to maintain those records until ... well, death or, at least, until a matter is fully litigated. If your husband will not keep records, you will need to do it.

Don't be caught off-guard if the ex sues your husband for child support already paid, perhaps in the hope your husband doesn't have proof of payment after many years. It is outlandish, evil and completely immoral for someone to sue for money they have received but would be entitled to if the payment record no longer exists. But you've got to face it – some people are outlandish, immoral and evil. So, it is better to keep the records. It may not stop a lawsuit, but it will shorten the argument when the ex's attorney receives copies of cancelled checks or other proof showing their client received the money.

Scrutinize and confirm every single claim and every piece of evidence.

If you have to check the weather yourself if the ex told you it was sunny, your husband will definitely want to verify *everything* the ex says or submits when it comes to the kid's expenses in setting child support. *Hold your horses there, Missy. Isn't there a chart based on the parents' income that courts use to determine child support?* That's a very good question, young grasshopper. There is, BUT, the chart is only a starting point for setting child support.

Say what?!

There's a whole lot more that goes into keeping a kid alive than just food, clothing and shelter. Courts take additional child rearing expenses into consideration when setting the child support amount. There's childcare, transportation for visitation, braces, sports, enhanced educational opportunities, prom dresses, prom tuxes, for that matter ... so many opportunities for a parent to spend money. And child support charts generally don't factor in nice-to-have expenses. The attorney for the receiving parent raises this. Da, da, da. There's that music again.

Additional expenses can sometimes be an ex's money maker. Imagine raking in an additional $100+ per month for many years and for expenses that may or may not exist. Take afterschool care, for example. Let's say you have a couple of kids the ex claims will require afterschool care while she works. Ok, makes sense. The cost is $200/month. Let's say mom and dad are to split the afterschool cost 50/50, with the ex's share on paper and dad writing a check to mom. With the kids in school nine months of the year, dad's share is $900 per year. Multiply that by ten years: $9,000.

But let's also say it's summer when this discussion takes place and the ex claims afterschool care begins when the kids start school in the Fall so she can't produce receipts. This also makes sense so your husband slaps his John Hancock on the document giving the ex an additional $900 per year. After the kids start school, your husband learns the kids aren't in afterschool care. But that doesn't mean he doesn't have to pay. There's a court order, after all. He would need to file a motion to modify, thus incurring perhaps thousands of dollars in legal fees ... unless he handles it himself. Provided he doesn't have to do this in another state. I'm tired just thinking about it.

How about another example? you ask.

OK. Let's say a court order has your husband responsible for reimbursing the ex 50% of what medical and dental insurance do not cover for the kid but only when the ex provides a bill and proof of payment to your husband within 30 days of the expense. Months, even years pass. Lives change and perhaps a new job, marriage for the ex, new insurance, lots going on. Because this book did not exist for this pair and they continue their post-divorce antics out of ignorance, they didn't know how to mitigate these minefields at the start and now find themselves back in court to discuss, among other things, a long unpaid dental bill the ex demands your husband reimburse.

As proof of bill and proof of payment, she submits an estimate from an Orthodontist for the kid's braces with a handwritten note of "dad's insurance doesn't cover" and an estimate of roughly $3,000. *Hmm*, your husband ponders. *Haven't seen these before. But wait, this is from* years *ago. It's not even a bill. And my insurance, then and now, covers orthodontia. Where's a cancelled check, debit receipt, credit card charge? What gives?*

At the hearing, with a lot of misdirection by the ex's attorney to confound the judge over the details (recall the ex is required to submit bill and proof of payment within 30 days to your husband or all bets are off), 50% of the $3,000 the ex wants appears to be getting the green light from the judge, even absent a bill and proof of payment. In the courtroom commotion, your husband's (imbecile, inept) attorney fails to point out to the judge that the bullshit document the ex offers as a bill and proof of payment isn't even close to a bill and is much farther away from being proof of payment. No bill, no proof of payment, ergo no payola to the ex. However, absent your husband's attorney spotlighting the couple's agreement and the ex's total failure to abide by that agreement, and, for all anyone knows, the judge may be playing Candy Crush behind the bench instead of paying attention to the details of your husband's case, this little detail may be lost on the judge and your husband could be saddled with an unnecessary $1,500 pay out to the ex who, in all likelihood, had the entire cost covered by her and her husband's insurance.

So, for every screwball claim the ex makes or evidence the ex proffers that intends to take more money out of your pockets, scrutinize the crap out of it and if there are discrepancies, your husband needs to point these out to his attorney. If in the middle of a hearing, then provide ***during the hearing***. This forces his attorney to confront the ex on her evidence. If the attorney refuses your husband's direction, your husband needs to immediately tell the judge that his attorney is refusing to do as he is instructing and needs to stop the proceedings instantly as he is firing his attorney.

Yeah, he can and needs to do that. Seriously. He's careening toward the edge of the Grand Canyon and isn't going to say a thing? And since most judges don't want to waste their or other's time if it is shown that an attorney is a real screw-up, they'll stop the whole damn thing in lieu of another hearing. If, on the other hand, the attorney does raise the discrepancies during the hearing and a judge still rules in the ex's favor, this would be the judge's mistake and opens the door to an appeal.

For other expenses, such as piano, dance or bungee jumping lessons, your husband needs to include in any order or agreement the conditions for the ex to receive additional monies and the **termination date** for any monies paid. If an order addresses multiple kids, and the order is silent on when expenses – e.g., afterschool care –terminate, the ex and the court will presume the money train for these expenses goes on until the *youngest* kid emancipates. Chew on that one!

To summarize:

1. Make the ex provide bona fide proof of an expense in accordance with the court order and if she can't produce rock solid evidence, pound home that point to a judge and don't let up until they cry "Uncle!"
2. Fire an attorney the moment you realize they don't know what the hell they're doing.
3. If an ex is unreliable, don't take her word that an expense will happen in the future while your husband pays in the present. If needed, include in any agreement, that your husband will pay only as long as the ex submits regular proof of payments for these expenses. No receipt. No moolah.

It's a lot to remember and a lot to catch when an ex tosses a lot of balls in the air during a hearing or in negotiations. But your husband must keep track if you are to save yourself bundles of cash in the long run.

As always, I'm keeping *my* eye on the ball for you, babe.

CHAPTER THREE

Kill All the Lawyers

I don't mean this literally, of course, and this is taken from Shakespeare, but should your husband find himself in a situation requiring legal representation, you will likely end up thinking it. Aside from the outrageous expense of an attorney's services, it has been my experience that many family law attorneys have little regard for the truth. (I can hear the uproar now from solicitors out there but you know what I'm talking about.) In fact, the more untruths they can insert into legal pleadings against the other party, the larger the fight. The larger the fight, the more you and your husband will pay. Of course, they will say they can't control their client's lying but once they discover their clients are little fibbers, how many actually rush to modify lie-littered pleadings? Uh ... zero.

In the 2014 documentary, *Divorce Corp.*, the filmmakers estimate that $50 billion (yes, billion, with a "b") is spent by families each year on divorce, child custody and support matters. The family court system actually incentivizes attorneys to prolong litigation until the divorcing/feuding parents' assets dry up and can no longer fund attorney fees, of which, according to the filmmakers, a portion of collected fees goes toward electing family court judges to color a judge's ruling – in favor of the contributing attorneys.

As sinister as that sounds, even in cases where attorneys are not well connected to judges, the siren song of lots of cash may be difficult to resist. So, where is the harm in an attorney encouraging a client-mother to claim the father has not paid child support for many years, even though there hadn't been a peep out of the mother during those years? All that will happen is the father will be required to produce cancelled checks or other evidence that may or may not be acceptable to the Court to show he did pay child support.

If dad is unable to rustle up the cancelled checks from a decade or more past, oh well. He will just have to pay the ex again. Her attorney can also charge for issuing subpoenas to demand production of cancelled checks, calculate and charge for totaling of cancelled checks, have multiple discussions with the father's attorney about alleged child support arrears and/or cancelled checks, request and attend a deposition to question the father and, possibly, you about the cancelled checks, demand the father be put into jail for not having years' worth of cancelled checks … the opportunities to invoice clients are endless.

While an ex may delight in the treatment of her ex and his wife, the possibility of the ex receiving a windfall if your husband cannot produce cancelled checks, is only short lived. After all, the mother will have to incur legal fees for her attorney issuing subpoenas to demand production of cancelled checks, calculating and charging for totaling of cancelled checks, having multiple discussions with the father's attorney about alleged child support arrears and/or cancelled checks, requesting and attending a deposition to question the father and, possibly, you about the cancelled checks, demanding the father be put into jail for not having years' worth of cancelled checks and so on. It is a lot like Las Vegas but without any chance of beating the house. Whatever monies the ex may "win," she returns directly to her attorney in the form of legal fees. Can you see how this is a game? Like in the movie, *War Games*, the best way to win the game is to avoid playing it in the first place.

But, as much as you hope your husband will not ever need to hire a lawyer, should there come a time when he does, you will want to know the following tips. This is by no means legal advice and I am not an attorney, but it is knowledge I wish I had from the beginning.

Never write a child support check to the mother on behalf of your husband.

This was my first suggestion for a reason. If your signature is on the checks, you risk being called in for a deposition or questioned at a hearing if you have had anything whatsoever to do with writing child support checks, especially when child support arrears is a topic of discussion at the hearing. If you do not ever write a check to the ex, you will be one less vehicle the attorneys can use to run up their fees.

Make your husband explain to you any strategy his attorney recommends before the lawyer files any document in a lawsuit.

Every battle begins with a strategy. And make no mistake, if your husband finds himself in a lawsuit, it is a battle. When the Germans attacked Poland, kicking off World War II, the Germans didn't just wake up on the wrong side of the bed one morning and then wing it. To win a battle means you need a strategy. And a winning strategy all the better.

In my experience, most family law attorneys do not employ a strategy in child custody and support cases. They don't weigh outcomes before filing the pivotal document that kick starts the war. They file some document and then wait to see what the responding party returns before deciding their next step. That is not only *no* strategy, that is a *bad* strategy and one that is extremely detrimental to your husband.

If your husband cannot tell you his attorney's strategy or doesn't understand the strategy, send him straight back to the attorney's office and make him stay there until he does understand it or until the attorney gives him a strategy and one that considers the Big Picture.

And *what is the Big Picture,* you ask?

The Big Picture is seeing the future of the kids and their parents. Perhaps the kids are toddlers now but at some point, they will want to take piano lessons, need braces, play sports, attend a formal school dance, drive a car, or go to college. All this stuff costs money. And it is important that both parents plan for these events. For parents, there may be remarriage, a move, sometimes to another state or country, a job change or loss, and even death while the children are still minors. This makes up the Big Picture.

There is no reason, however, your husband cannot consider these events in the very first court order and, failing that, in a single subsequent order. There is no legal requirement that parents return to court year-over-year to get more money for expected and unexpected events. Shit happening is a reasonable expectation for all parents – including attorneys, who are likely parents themselves. There is no excuse for not considering many of life's possibilities when hammering out the details in the very first court order. The only reason divorcing couples don't consider the Big Picture is that their attorneys have zero incentive to consider the Big Picture because, come on, they want you as a returning customer.

Unfortunately, in my experience, the time horizon for most attorneys seems to be what is happening in the moment as though how it is today is how it will be ten or more years in the future. When there is a substantial change of circumstances in the lives of kids and their parents, this invariably involves a return visit to the court to revise the agreements. This is utter nonsense and a conspiracy to separate parents from their money.

In my husband's first child support and visitation agreement at his divorce, when the children were just 1½ and 3 years old, the attorneys, in their incredibly myopic sight, laid out visitation for a 1½ and 3-year-old, when their daily schedule consisted of playing, eating, sleeping. They also thought it was a brilliant idea for the parents, who were quite acrimonious toward one another, to divide visitation during the summer without defining specific dates. This was a particularly intelligent move by the attorneys, especially when one of the children's birthday occurs in July. Summer visitation was great, way back when (she writes with a smirk).

You may also recall from Chapter Two how my husband inadvertently agreed to pay childcare costs until his children graduated college. This is a prime example of an attorney who failed to see the Big Picture but, more accurately, was purely incompetent.

Have your husband fire his attorney if the attorney won't provide a strategy.

Devising a strategy to win the case is an attorney's job, for crying out loud. If they fail at this, trust they will fail at successfully resolving whatever issue is before the Court. And it is incredibly easy to fire an attorney. All your husband has to do is go Donald Trump on the attorney by saying, "You're fired." The attorney then files a Motion to Withdraw as Counsel with the Court. Your husband then finds himself another, hopefully, more competent attorney.

Scrutinize the attorney's invoices.

In the 1990's movie, *The Firm*, Tom Cruise played Mitch McDeere, an attorney at a small, but ultra-successful Memphis law firm. The Firm owed its success to representing members of the Mob that McDeere discovers after learning of the untimely deaths of some of the Firm's associates. The U.S. government asks McDeere for his assistance in nailing the Firm's partners and, in the process, the Mob, by Mitch revealing confidential client information. Having taken an oath to maintain client confidentiality, helping the government would, ironically, result in McDeere losing his license to practice law. What to do?

Quite by chance, a non-Mob client questions McDeere about invoices he has been receiving from the Firm. He tells McDeere the Firm has been overcharging clients for years (*Why did he wait so long to complain?* this author wonders) and advises him that each time the Firm mailed an inflated invoice they were breaking the law. A lightbulb goes off for McDeere. He reviews the Firm's time sheets against client invoices and discovers the Firm has been overcharging every client, including the Mob. The penalties for this infraction are stiff and something the government can now use to take down the Firm without Mitch dishonoring the oath he took. And, of course, leaving the Mob firmly in place to do their thing.

For some family law attorneys, this is life imitating art. Would you believe some attorneys charge for things they do not do, flood their pleadings with falsehoods that require additional litigation or charge such excessive amounts for simple actions it makes you convinced the attorney is high? One of my husband's attorneys charged him for preparing a Summary Judgment (a judgment entered by a Court for one party and against another party without a full trial), that was never filed and was, from what we could tell, not connected to what was going on at that time. No explanation, just a line item on the monthly invoice. This same attorney billed my husband hundreds of dollars for arranging depositions for out-of-state witnesses and preparing/sending subpoenas – all without my husband's knowledge – and then, equally inexplicably, cancelled all of it. We only discovered it when she sent her invoice. Criminal. And that attorney is still out there, practicing law.

And nearly every one of my husband's attorneys have invoiced him lavish amounts for conducting *research*. Yes, billing thousands of dollars for knowledge they claim necessary to handle his case – despite claiming possession of this knowledge when enticing him to become a client.

Sadly, there may be little solace knowing your husband's ex is in the same boat with her attorney. My husband's last big appearance in court included defending against an allegation of not having paid child support for ten years prior to the kids moving to our house. After producing stacks of cancelled checks to prove otherwise, the ex's attorney then sought reimbursement of legal fees from my husband, to include $13,000+ for their paralegal to total the cancelled checks; monies claimed to not have been received by the ex. (And the judge and my husband's attorney couldn't see the irony in that?) Adding insult to injury seems to be a favorite pastime for some attorneys.

At an hourly rate of $150 or so for the paralegal, alone, $13,000+ would amount to 86-some hours – *more than two business weeks* – to add up approximately 150 or so pieces of paper. I am no paralegal but I imagine I could probably accomplish this in less than one hour (probably a lot less) with a calculator. Were I the ex, I would have definitely lost it over that charge.

The moral of the story: Pay attention to what an attorney charges. Question everything and if the attorney has a difficult time explaining anything on those invoices, go Mitch McDeere on them. It is against the law to falsify or embellish invoices. The attorney could lose their license and go to jail, and should, if cheating their clients.

Have your husband prepare good questions to ask attorneys before he hires one.

Do you remember the last time you went for a job interview? Were you asked a lot of questions about your ability to do the job? Were you asked to prove, by example or otherwise, that you could do the job? Did you have to speak to several people at the company, who also asked you many of the same questions? Did they ask for and check your references? Did they conduct a thorough background check or have you take a drug test?

Companies take these steps even if the job pays $10 per hour. Yet, people hire attorneys who charge $350+ per hour and only *assume* the attorney can and will do the job. With attorney fees in child support and custody cases costing parents $5,000-$100,000 or more, you would think everyone would grasp the importance of determining if the attorney is even qualified to do the job. As in any profession, there are more and less qualified people. The legal community is no different. Having a law degree and license is no guarantee of competence. Consider there is always someone at the bottom of the class.

You also need to be mindful of attorneys who charge *you* to interview *them*. It is as if possessing a law degree automatically confers unquestionable expertise. I am here to tell you – it does not. Whenever I have had to employ an attorney for business issues, I viewed them for what they are: a contractor, someone who works for me – not the other way around. If I am paying, I want to make sure they are sufficiently skilled to do the job. And it starts with *my* interviewing *them*. And I don't pay for that.

So, here are some starter questions for your husband to ask an attorney when interviewing them for the job:

1. How many cases like mine have you handled?
Tell me about them. A child support/custody case is rarely the same from case to case. The attorney should be able to explain similarities and the outcomes of those cases. If they cannot, advise your husband to keep shopping.

2. What is your current caseload?
During the course of a two-year representation, my husband's former attorney filed lawsuits on behalf of approximately 40 other clients. That

meant the attorney was managing a zillion details for at least 40 people, my husband included. She likely was also courting new clients to fill her pipeline and in the process of filing even more lawsuits. However, it was only her and a part-time paralegal at her law firm so, naturally, many things were going to, and did, slip through the cracks.

So, your husband needs to evaluate the lay of the land. Too many cases and too few people at the law firm to do the work means something is going to suffer – and it will likely be your husband's case. This is especially important to keep in mind if believing a busy lawyer = competent lawyer. That is a possibility, but attorneys are (somewhat) human and can only handle so much. To determine an attorney's workload, you can check your local family court's online system and, if possible, search by the attorney's name to see the number of cases they currently have in play.

3. Tell me about your trial experience.

I believe many caught up in the family law system are woefully ignorant of what is truly happening. The document filed with the court, by either or both sides, that kick starts the mayhem, is a *lawsuit*. It is not just a vehicle for enhanced discussion about money or the kids. Filing a lawsuit means someone is being sued. If your husband is on the receiving end, the ex is suing him. It is important to understand this. And it will only be resolved by agreement or a Judge unless the ex abandons the suit altogether. If your husband and ex cannot agree on how to resolve the dispute, the matter will go before a Judge and the Judge will decide – after a trial.

Prior to trial, the attorneys will collect evidence to support their client's position and/or dispel the opposing party's position. This is called "discovery." Often, when there is enough evidence to support or dispel a position, the parties will concede to an agreement. From there, the Agreed Order, or similarly titled document, is drawn up, the parties sign, and the Agreed Order is filed with the Court. The parties are then bound to conduct themselves according to the Agreed Order.

If no agreement, then a trial.

Understanding that an honest-to-goodness trial is a very real possibility in any lawsuit can better guide your husband in his selection of an attorney as the attorney he hires had better have solid trial experience. While you may believe an attorney having trial experience is just part of the lawyer package, that isn't necessarily so with all attorneys. It is critical your husband ask prospective attorneys about their trial experience because lawyers who lack this experience or are just plain awful at litigating can undermine your husband's case – even if the evidence is in your husband's favor. In yet a second Tom Cruise film reference, that of *A Few Good Men*, Kevin Pollak, as Lieutenant Sam Weinberg, tells Demi Moore's character, another attorney, "You object once, so we can say he's not a criminologist. If you keep after it, it looks like a bunch of fancy lawyer tricks. It's the difference between paper law and trial law."

And there is a huge difference between the two.

One other thing to understand on this topic: the law is about logic. It is about presenting evidence in such a way that there is a logical conclusion. If an attorney lacks this expertise, run.

4. How much research will you need to conduct and why will you need to conduct research? Will you agree, in writing, to a maximum amount that you will charge for research?

Remember, folks, attorneys are to be *experienced* professionals and, from experience, should already possess, at the minimum, basic family law knowledge. There may be some nuances to your husband's case that requires the attorney to locate precedents or a law for an unusual circumstance, but when an attorney tells your husband there is no limit on what they will charge for research, your husband must keep shopping.

5. How do you invoice? Will you charge me for every paperclip, copy, telephone call I make to you – even after hearing nothing from you for weeks – emails I send about your invoice, weekly case meetings, etc.?

The possibilities for charging a client are exhaustive.

Another former attorney for my husband provided an estimate of $10,000 to appeal a ruling from a lower court after his former 40-client+ attorney screwed up big time. The Appellate Court prescribes the process so Appellate attorneys know exactly what they can and cannot do and what to expect from the opposing party. So, when a second invoice for $8,000 arrived after consuming the $10,000 retainer, a big red light went off. Then another $8,000 invoice one month later. Sirens are now blaring. How could an experienced Appellate attorney be so far off in her estimate when nothing unexpected had happened? She, reluctantly, agreed to "write-off" the difference between her estimate and her invoices.

Another attorney, over the course of six months, invoiced my husband $87.50 each time they retrieved his file from a filing cabinet, another $87.50 for discussing my husband's case during the firm's weekly meetings, and an additional $87.50 to return the file to the file cabinet. (They charged in 15-minute increments, even if it took 30 seconds.) I kid you not. And not once during those six months of retrieving and discussing the contents of that amazing folder did the attorney file the motion for which my husband hired him to file. In total, $6,300 for moving a manila folder around their office. To add further insult, when my husband asked the attorney why he did not file the motion for which he was retained, the attorney could not explain but charged him $175 for asking. And this was a firm specializing in father's rights. Right.

Evaluate if your husband needs a lawyer.

You and/or your husband may only think he needs a lawyer whenever he is served with a lawsuit by the ex or the ex decides court orders are merely suggestions. It's entirely possible your husband can handle the matter without any legal representation. Considering the experiences my husband has had with attorneys, he would have been better off financially and would not have fared any worse than had he not retained counsel. While I am certain the thought of "going it alone" may be a bit frightening, there are some very good programs out there that teach people how to handle their own cases without incurring those outrageous legal fees.

I know, I know. As the proverb goes, every man who is his own lawyer, has a fool for a client. However, considering that my husband's attorney missed the whole daycare-costs-until-the-children-graduated-college-thing, another attorney left him responsible for paying into savings accounts absent any conditions, set-up the parents for a Battle Royale each summer over visitation and so many other errors and oversights, really, how much worse could he have done if he was on his own?

If you see monies going out the door to your husband's attorney but no movement, tell your husband to fire the attorney.

Some attorneys will purposely stall your case so they can attend to other cases and may even charge your husband for doing a little something, like research or moving his file around the office, to make it appear something is happening, but not getting the case any closer to resolution. This is bad.

My husband's 40+-client attorney stalled his case for months as she took on a monstrous caseload and didn't have time for his. She lied about the courts being backed up and being unable to get the case set for trial. Meanwhile, the ex's attorney filed a motion in court to force my husband to move things along, with, astoundingly, my husband threatened to be penalized for his attorney's inaction.

If your husband doesn't take action against lazy or ineffective attorneys, the court will see this as your husband condoning the stall and there could be additional penalties – to your husband. In that case, have your husband line up another attorney or prepare to go it alone and then fire the offending attorney.

Have your husband obtain an estimate from the attorney at the start and then monitor the charges.

This just makes good sense yet many people miss this. In fact, people will invest more time getting an estimate from their auto mechanic – and holding them to it – than they will an attorney. Unless you want some big surprises, make your husband get an estimate and keep tabs on what the attorney disburses from the retainer or is charging. Encourage your husband to keep regular communication with his attorney about fees, especially if he sees the retainer erode and there appears a lot left to accomplish. If the attorney's invoices are out of control, unless something unusual happened en route, have your husband question the attorney as to why their estimate is inaccurate and have him demand they correct.

Keep in mind that an attorney, like a plumber or electrician, is in business. And like a plumber or electrician, attorneys need happy customers, for repeat business, referrals, and good reviews. Your husband is a *customer* of the attorney, not a hostage. This means your husband has the upper hand.

Your husband can (and should) refuse to pay for sub-standard legal services.

The attorney will likely resist, but if an attorney is, say, sitting in negotiations knitting or appears bewildered by the whole case, your husband did not agree to pay for this and needs to demand a credit to the retainer or not to be charged. Should there be a concern his attorney will dump him, leaving him high and dry in the middle of a fight if he questions the attorney, know that a disgruntled attorney cannot just fire a client without taking specific steps in accordance with the American Bar Association's Model Rules of Professional Conduct and/or local Court rules. So, no, attorneys don't have the upper-hand – unless they are unethical.

One way for your husband to protect himself from an unscrupulous attorney or ineffective representation is to charge his retainer or legal fees to a credit card. Should the attorney charge him for something they did not do, invoices questionable amounts, or fails to do the job at all, have your husband dispute the charge with his credit card company. The credit card company will go to the merchant (the attorney) and ask them to support the charges made. If the attorney cannot or will not, the credit card company will credit those monies back to your husband's credit card account.

From experience, I can tell you that when my husband disputed a credit card charge when an attorney failed to perform the invoiced services, the attorney did not respond to the credit card company and the credit card company credited his account. Too much work for the attorney to defend their position, I suppose.

CHAPTER FOUR

In-laws and Other "Family"

This can be one heck of a touchy subject. For starters, your in-laws are now your family and you likely want to create or maintain harmony because this can be a very long relationship. I also believe the majority of subsequent wives truly hope their new family will grow to love and accept them, as she hopes to reciprocate, especially when they see their son/brother/cousin/nephew so doggone happy because of her. And, in some cases, this does happen. I know. I've actually seen in-laws embrace a new daughter-in-law (and, sometimes, even her children). It is a wonderful sight.

Unfortunately, there are some in-laws who cling to your husband's ex regardless of the torment she inflicts on their son, new daughter-in-law, and grandchildren. And it goes without saying that your stepkids, even if they were to burn down your house or steal your car, will probably always be golden with the in-laws while you, eh, maybe not so much.

It is difficult to understand why an in-law would prefer a morally deficient ex to a subsequent wife who sacrifices plenty for her husband and his children. It is equally impossible to comprehend why some in-laws would assign the cause of their family's decades-long angst, in and amongst themselves, to a new wife and pander to an ex while blowing off the new wife when, oh, I don't know, perhaps her parent dies or she experiences some other personal tragedy. Passive aggressive much?

People can be funny creatures.

And if dealing with in-laws isn't challenging enough, you may soon discover that "family" is not limited solely to your in-laws. The family I am referring to is the *ex's* family. Yep, there could be a mother, father, siblings, siblings' spouses, siblings' children, aunts, uncles – people related by blood to your stepchildren, their relatives, the people your stepchildren love, no matter what. And they can be a whole cadre of people who may have it in for you for no other reason than the ex doesn't much care for you. Yep, there are a whole lot of people that have potential to cause you grief.

Tough as it may be, there are ways to manage your emotions when it comes to dealing with all these "family" members, without incurring negative consequences.

Accept that your in-laws' allegiance may be to the ex.

Understand that you came second, third or whenever and even if the ex cheated, lied, and stole from your husband, your husband's family may still hold the ex in higher esteem than they do you. This usually happens for a couple of reasons: 1) They don't want to jeopardize their relationship with the kids by shunning the ex and/or 2) They also may have a long relationship with the ex that hasn't been tainted in the same way as it has with your husband (and they run a little short on empathy).

Your husband's family may give the appearance of compassion for your husband's troubles with the ex, and, heck, some in-laws may be even catty about the ex, but unless the ex did something directly to your in-laws, pseudo-empathy may be all your husband gets. That's because your in-laws didn't feel the sting of infidelity, miss watching their children grow up or have to pay thousands of dollars in attorney fees to enforce Court orders. Nope. Your in-laws have had and will have an entirely differently experience with the ex.

Too, being the new wife doesn't compel people to dismiss long-standing relationships. The best advice, purely to save your own sanity, is to accept it for what it is. Really. I understand that you would love it if your husband set his family straight, but there isn't much you can do if your in-laws favor maniacs. Just like in grade school, there were kids who liked you and kids who did not. But that didn't stop you from advancing in life. Neither should this if your in-laws favor the ex.

Accept that your in-laws' allegiance is to the ex and kids instead of your husband.

You may come to terms with your in-laws favoring the ex and kids over *you*. But, your in-laws favoring the ex and the kids over *your husband* may really irk you. As previously noted, it may terrify the in-laws that if they are less warm to the ex, the ex will keep them away from the kids. Of course, if your husband sees the kids regularly, they could see them when they are with him but sometimes that doesn't compute with grandparents. It may also be that the idea of conflict is so frightening to them, they wouldn't dare say a thing to a malicious ex. I am only an observer, not a psychologist, so please take my theories with a grain of salt.

Also, for some in-laws, no matter what the kids do to their dad or to you, because the kid is blood, as long as the kid doesn't do something dastardly to your in-laws, the kids will always win out and your in-laws will always be able to justify taking the kid's side over yours.

Accept unequal treatment on your birthday and/or at holidays.

There may be in-laws who look forward to occasions such as holidays or birthdays to exercise their passive-aggressive muscles. It may be that your in-laws insist you celebrate holidays at their house, exclusively, or that at Christmas, there is a distinct 10-1 ratio of gifts for family members – them, 10, you, 1. Perhaps your in-laws send a sizable check in their Christmas card, with the check made out only to your husband. Your birthday goes unnoticed while your husband's sibling madly texts your husband, a grown man, to call their mother on her birthday – even though the day is young, and you've already lavished your mother-in-law with gifts.

These may be just the occasions your in-laws wait for each year to demonstrate how they really feel about you. Let it go, as you cannot change other people. If you don't, it will steal your life from you. Concentrate on those who truly love you, not people who don't. I am not saying that it won't eat you up a bit as it will. But suppress you must as people who pull this shit on others are not happy people. And you don't have the ability to make them happy. So, count your blessings that there are others in your life who do love you. That's where you put your focus.

Be prepared for your gifts to your in-laws to be dismissed (or discarded).

You scoured the shops of Madrid to find just the right anniversary gift for your in-laws and gingerly transport a silver bowl rimmed in mother-of-pearl back to the U.S. You can't wait to hear their reaction. A simple note arrives, thanking you for the "bowl" that you later find tossed in the back of a bottom cabinet in their vacation home. You find a rare gem set in 18K gold earrings that are perfect for your mother-in-law's milestone birthday. They are a little pricey but this day comes only once in a lifetime so you spring for it. You never see the earrings again.

If you find your in-laws do not appreciate the gifts you give, stop giving nice gifts. An inexpensive scarf or watch, or, essentially, anything that doesn't take up too much of your time or money is entirely adequate for those who are unappreciative. This goes for all ingrates you know, not just in-laws.

The first time you take this stand you may feel a little uneasy, believing they will realize you're altering your gift giving. You may even fear they see this as retaliation against their bad behavior. To that I say, *don't worry about it*. If they don't care about your feelings, why spend gobs of time and cash on them, only opening the door for another insult? Are you crazy? Insecure? What?

By sending something, anything, regardless of what it is, you still maintain the social contract but now get to keep the money you would have typically spent on a nicer gift. And that will be a nice gift to yourself.

Keep your distance from those other "family" members.

You may have the pleasure (she writes, tongue in cheek) of interacting with the ex's family. And make no mistake – the ex's family will cross your path at some time in your life. We're talking graduations, birthdays, holidays, weddings, births, deaths … essentially all occasions the kids would attend. Understand, though, that even if the ex's family appears friendly toward you, if there is ever a rift between your husband and his ex, those same people will likely turn on you, slander you, lie about obtaining restraining orders against your husband after helping the ex violate Court-ordered visitation, and may not hesitate to lie about you and your husband in Court if it will further the ex's cause.

Best advice: Keep your distance from the ex's family no matter how congenial they may appear to be at the start. They are likely being nice because they are curious about you, not because they are interested in your life or well-being. You don't need to be brash about remaining distant; just remain in the background.

However, if any of the ex's family members are nasty or disrespectful to you, you are under no obligation to be nice to them or invite them to any function you may have for the kid. For instance, say your stepkid lives with you, is graduating from high school and you want to celebrate the moment. The ex doesn't want to participate in the planning of the event and also doesn't want to go out of her way for her own kid unless her plans can upset yours. So, you invite your husband's family, your friends, and the ex's family for a brunch to celebrate. The ex and her mother show up late and her mother greets everyone at the table except you. The ex's mother then sits down to a $50 per plate brunch you and your husband are hosting and departs the same way she came in – without a word. The ex's mother may be an elderly woman and your parents may have raised you properly so you remain gracious in this ignorance.

Well, there's no need to be gracious going forward. She doesn't get any more invites and you don't need to acknowledge her presence ever again. This is not to say you go out of your way so the ex's ignorant family member understands you are ignoring or excluding them. You simply don't invite them to anything – ever – and it is not necessary to acknowledge them in any significant way the next time your paths cross. They will understand your intentions, and the reasons behind them, but, hey, it's not like their being left off your guest list or you ignoring them will re-start their acrimony toward you.

Alternatively, especially if you're the gregarious type, and just to throw everyone off kilter, when your paths cross, welcome them with widespread arms, a big hug and a comment of how absolutely wonderful they look. Their confusion will linger long after the event.

CHAPTER FIVE
Disciplining the Kiddies: Who's in Charge Here?

Please don't let the brevity of this chapter mislead you into believing that disciplining stepkids is a no-brainer. They misbehave, you yell, spank, put in them time out or whatever your parents did to you and/or you do to your own kids. Slow down there, Missy, 'cause it ain't that cut and dry.

You and your husband have set house rules the kids are to follow but, guess what? Kids (your own included) don't always follow rules and sometimes do some pretty stupid stuff that may warrant discipline, if not jail time. You were once a kid so it should not come as a shock when a stepkid does something outside the rules.

But, seeing yourself as a level-headed woman with a good upbringing, you believe you have a pretty good idea of how to discipline children who misbehave. For stepmoms with their own children, you will most definitely have your own discipline style and what may be good for your own offspring surely should be good enough for the offspring of your husband and his ex, correct?

I don't think so.

I know many stepparents who believe they are free to discipline stepkids, with some looking forward to showing them who is boss. I could not disagree more. You disciplining your stepkid will just piss off the kids and, guess who else? That's right – the ex. Consider you were probably suspect to begin with so when the kid reports to their mom that you've disciplined them, expect wrath coming your way.

But wait, you may say. *All I did was take little Jimmy by the arm and place him in a chair for 15 minutes for beating up his brother.* However, that's not the story that will be told to mom. (You do know kids are fantastic storytellers, right?) In little Jimmy's version, you, without any provocation whatsoever, stormed into his room, applied a vice-like grip on his frail little arm until it was throbbing, dragged him down the hallway on his back and down the stairs, his tiny little head slamming against each step, where you then flung him into a chair, nearly crushing his spine, and then duct taped him so he couldn't see, talk or move for eight hours.

Because the ex probably already thinks you are evil, to her, the story is completely plausible. She earmarks it to be included in the next lawsuit should your husband request an increase in visitation or will lay into you or your husband about how you have zero business laying one finger on the kid. And it doesn't need to be that fantastical of a story. Anything you do that even *slightly* smacks of punishment can become lawsuit filler.

For example, you could insist the children eat only healthy meals in your house, of which the kids resist as they are accustomed to a diet of hotdogs and cereal at mom's. You tell the children that your well-balanced meal is all they will have for that meal and if they choose not to eat, they're going to be hungry. You feel quite proud of yourself for demonstrating the importance of eating healthy meals though a 6-year-old not weaned off weenies probably won't see it the same way. And mom probably won't as well. In fact, you later find the ex's accusations in a lawsuit filed against your husband that you "starve" the kids. Really? Starve? And where's dad in all of this child abuse? It's interesting how a lot of these stories have dad nowhere to be found while stepmom is left alone to torture the kiddies.

Regardless of any backlash you may receive from the ex, it just isn't a great idea to discipline other people's children, especially when, in most cases, they have two parents. Of course, if kids endanger themselves, you need to take swift action to save them from themselves, but spanking, grounding or putting them in time out is their parents' domain. Why is this good for you? Just imagine a life where when your stepkid talks to their mom and others about you, they only have good things to say. That'll probably also piss off mom but you be can be assured the feel-good stories won't make it into a lawsuit.

So, if this didn't make it clear, here are more words of caution on the topic of discipline.

DON'T. THAT'S IT. DON'T.

Don't discipline your stepkids. Period. No discussion. No rationalization. Nothing. Don't do it, don't even contemplate it. Let their parents discipline *their* children. Got that? *Their* children. Not yours. You're free to discipline your own children as are your stepkid's parents. This is not to suggest you should ignore a stepkid attempting something dangerous while in your care but dishing out consequences is better left to their parents.

Naturally, you can and should rat out the stepkids to their parents when they're out of line, but if you institute the discipline, you would be a fool to think the kids will later look back on your discipline as being a good thing and something that made them a better person. Well, forget about it. If you raise your voice or your hand to the stepkid, they will in all likelihood, resent the hell out of you for sticking your nose into something that doesn't concern you – namely, their bad behavior that is to be corrected by biological parents.

I'll give you an example. Let's say you are home alone with the stepkids. You learn one of the kids has pushed the button on the garage door opener so many times that the garage door opener catches fire. Instead of banishing him to his room, taking away his video games, or denying him food and water, instead, you tell his father. While the repairman is replacing the garage door opener, the same stepkid is up in his room throwing stuffed animals into an overhead fan to disable it. Again, you advise dad so he can determine the appropriate discipline.

Because you did not put anyone in timeout, spank, or scream, you are then viewed by the kids as being nice. And because you didn't take any of the aforementioned disciplinary actions, the stepkids have nada to report to mom. Happy ending.

Conversely, let's consider a stepfather slapping his 7-year-old stepkid for failing to dress quickly. That pisses off the stepkid who reports the slapping to your husband who then loses it and proceeds to make it a nightmare for the stepfather until the stepfather can't take it anymore and splits. Maybe the stepkids are just fine with stepdad leaving but if the ex had been focusing her energy on that husband and now he's out of the picture, guess who now is the recipient of her attention? Do you see where I am going with this?

I'll change it up a bit for pre-stepmoms:

Pay attention to how your fiancé disciplines his kids before getting married.

If like many women in love, you're convinced the guy who allows his children to get away with murder before you are married will suddenly develop extraordinary parenting skills post-nuptials. Or the little rascal, the one who let out a blood curdling scream in Taco Bell after discovering cheese in his burrito, that caused Taco Bell patrons to suffer cardiac arrest, will suddenly be an exemplary citizen after you walk the aisle. If your fiancé sucks at parenting and his toddler is a nightmare during courtship, consider this scenario magnified ten times, maybe more, when it is occurring in your house and you have nowhere to escape. Is this what you envisioned for your marriage? Probably not.

If this sounds familiar, either get your intended into some sort of parenting program or you may want to re-imagine your future; one where you are pulling out your hair as your stepkid pours chocolate sauce on your white sofa with your husband assuring you this is just a phase or the other, where you are contentedly lounging on a tropical beach with your new, childless, husband on your honeymoon. Your choice, honey, because a signature on a piece of paper only changes things at the IRS.

CHAPTER SIX

When the Kids Come a Callin'

Shortly after I married, the ex sticking to the visitation schedule became, let's say, *challenging*. A seasoned stepmom advised she had the same issue with her third husband's ex-wife (I know – excessive) continually ignoring the Court-ordered visitation schedule or making repeated requests to change the schedule. My friend simply picked up the phone, dialed the ex-wife, and said, "Stick to the order."

My friend reported this event without an ounce of emotion as though recalling placing a phone order for a pizza. I asked if the ex-wife abided by her instruction. There was some vague claim the ex had and, for a moment, I didn't doubt it because there was something a little threatening beneath my friend's icy exterior. I don't know if the ex-wife actually complied with my friend's demand but one thing I concluded from this is: Don't let anything about visitation get to *you*.

Recall this book is for *you*, dear girl.

I realized, many years later, that my friend didn't really care that much about her third husband having ongoing contact with his children; not that she was heartless, well, maybe a little, but she was powerless to control others. Besides, my friend was busy with her own children, her own visitation schedules with her exs and her career. She didn't have time to fix or fret about visitation issues between her husband and his ex. Husbands are adults and should handle this on their own. And that, sweet girl, is the key to maintaining your sanity should the ex use the children's visits with their dad as a weapon against your husband.

Please don't misunderstand. I wholeheartedly believe it is vital kids spend time with both parents unless a parent is psychotic. Absent psychosis, this generally means shuttling kids back and forth between two homes where, likely, there are different rules, traditions, people, pets and so on that can and do disrupt the kiddies' equilibrium. I can only imagine the confusion *I* might suffer had my mom allowed me to be a slob and disrespectful, because that's what fun parents do but, because my dad wants me to function among civilized human beings, rudeness and sloppiness are *verboten*. Different houses, different rules, different lifestyles sucks for kids. Not to mention, it can be confusing as hell.

Beyond creating, potentially, neurotic kids, shared custody has the potential to screw up your life as well. As I wrote previously, I am a huge believer that kids need to spend time with both parents – even if you think the ex is Satan incarnate. I also believe visitation should not be used as a tool to punish or coerce a non-custodial parent into doing what the ex wants, but have heard far too many stories, and experienced a few of our own, to know the whole visitation thing can suck some seriously precious time from your life. As I promised at the outset, this book intends only to open your eyes to potential problems and things you may wish to consider to maintain *your* mental well-being if/when you see things going off the rails – and possibly careening off a cliff. Yikes.

So, pay attention, honey, as I'm about to save you a lot of agony and likely quite a few bucks.

Review your fiancé's shared custody order *before* marrying.

As mentioned in Chapter Two, it is important you know what you're getting into when marrying a man with children and how time and money in your new marriage will be/is controlled by some legal agreement your fiancé is required to follow. A shared custody agreement is no exception.

You may believe that after you marry, your life will continue as before but only better. You may be walking around in a daze still believing your budget will continue to allow you to fly across country to visit your family each year or indulge in your annual trip to the Bahamas. Not so fast, cowgirl. The shared custody order probably has some other plans in store for you, especially if the order requires dad to transport his children to and fro' the ex six times per year and it isn't just around the block. And, although your fiancé might not readily admit it, your appearance on the scene or, more likely, the appearance of your income, may have him gasping a sigh of financial relief as he continues to boost his *children's* frequent flyer accounts.

So, read the shared custody agreement, discuss it with your intended, and see if you can live with it. If you can't, well, a legal document requiring *you* to be there has not yet been created.

Nothin' is etched in stone.

Even if you read, reviewed and decided you could live with your fiancé's shared custody schedule, it can change and often does – especially when the ex just can't seem to make up her mind on which husband to stay married to or where to live. Family court exists for a reason and one of those reasons is to allow the constant changing of custody schedules whenever mom gets some wild idea to move the children, enrolls the kids in a year-round versus traditional school, and perhaps back again, with the custody schedule suddenly obsolete and requiring a brand-new order. And, by new order, I mean, a lengthy, expensive legal battle, if dad complains about the ex's roller coaster.

And don't discount influence from the ex's boyfriends and subsequent husbands in the shaping of the custody schedule. As it often happens, once the ex moves onto someone else, the importance of your husband in the kid's life is no longer, shall we say … important? At least in the eyes of the ex and wannabe daddys. And that means the ex will have to figure out how to reduce time the kids spend with their dad to appease the ex's latest love interest.

Understand that to the ex, her new love is everything your husband was not. As such, she believes the children also see their father as she does and feels the kids are better off spending more time with husbands two, three or four than they would with their father. After all, number two (or beyond) is now the "new" dad, she may proclaim, because after countless court-sanctioned moves far away from dad or completely upending one shared custody schedule after another, dad is no longer able to remain involved in the children's day-to-day lives, like mom's new guy can. Duh.

This means only one thing to the ex: that damn shared custody order requires another revision. Naturally, it's total bullshit but hey, some people are just full of shit.

Meanwhile, back at the ranch, the kids are wondering, *whatever happened to that guy who was there since our birth? The guy we call 'dad'? And why is this new guy insisting we call him 'dad' and to forget about that other 'dad'?* Yeah, that won't have any psychological impact on a kid.

And moms who pull this crap wonder why their children act out. Big mystery, huh?

Court order requiring ex to provide transportation: Don't let her off the hook.

This is where you may want to get out your calculator.

Life can certainly be fluid. An ex often can and does meet their next soulmate, finds their next soul career or has a mother in another city, state, or country willing to babysit so the ex has ample time to locate her next soulmate or soul career without alerting your husband to how little time the kids are actually with her while your husband continues to pay her to support kids who are being provided for elsewhere. Holy cow. Where your husband once drove only three blocks to pick up his kids each week, the ex's court-approved move now puts serious mileage between the kids and your husband. It then can become all about *transporting* the kids to dad.

At first glance, driving the kids back and forth from the ex to your house may not seem like a big issue. I mean, what's the big deal about driving a couple of hundred miles, each way, two or three times per month? Well, let me tell you.

It sucks. Like in a major way. Consider the following.

Let's say you don't exceed the speed limit on highways. Right. And let's say the speed limit is 70 mph on the highway from your house to the ex and she lives 200 miles away. 200 miles/70 mph = 2.86 hours of drive time. One way. Now, multiply that by 4. That's correct, dear girl, as what goes up must also come down. Put simply – you gotta' drive 200 miles to get the kids, 200 miles back to your house and then another 400 miles, roundtrip, to return the kids and get your sorry, tired ass back home. That's 11.44 freakin' hours – in a car – for a weekend! That's like driving from

Los Angeles to Albuquerque, Chicago to Atlanta or Atlanta to Dallas. In fact, you could fly from L.A. to London in that amount of time. And you wouldn't even see a single movie.

Do this, minimally, once per month for, say, three years and that would be almost 2.5 **_weeks_**. 2.5 weeks of nothin' but staring at taillights with, perhaps, the added bonus of refereeing squabbling kids in the backseat because their mother decided their spending 5.72 or more hours in a car, at least once per month, for years on end, was the kindest thing she could inflict … er, I mean, *bestow* upon her children. Thanks, mom! Screw the homework we should probably be doing or getting to bed early for school the next day! Not us as we're hittin' the highways to accommodate mom's pursuit of free babysitting, a la granny, and outside of dad's view, now that we're 200 miles away. Mom. You. Are. The. Absolute. Best. We just can't wait until Mother's Day!

And if you think gas and wear and tear on a car is expensive, when kids take to the air, now we're talking serious dough. A couple of kids at an average of $400 each for plane fare, say, two times per year (and, really, who would move their kids so far away that the kids would only see their parent two times per year? I digress.) is $1,600. If you're thinking 1600 bucks a year ain't nuthin', put that money in an investment at a very conservative 6% over 10 years and it ain't so nuthin' now, is it?

Compound Interest Calculator

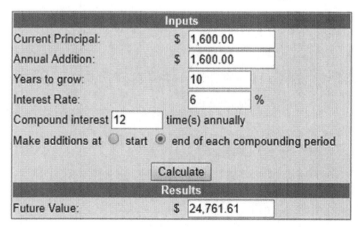

And for what? Because the ex doesn't want to incur the cost? Of course she doesn't. And neither should you and your husband.

So, if the ex's perpetual pursuit for self-satisfaction is the catalyst for ripping the kids from their dad, advise (threaten) your husband to make sure 1) The ex provides transportation and, 2) When she violates the agreement/order for not providing the transportation – I mean, come on, you think she will be overjoyed to spend 11.44 soul-sucking hours behind the wheel of a car or losing $25K? – hold her little Christian Louboutin-clad feet to the fire (of which you, too, could buy $800 shoes if not spending your money on assuming the ex's responsibility). And definitely make certain your husband does whatever is in his power to make sure the ex incurs the cost of all transportation. After all, her choice, her pain.

Won't lie to you here. The ex is gonna' fight and fight real hard. Remember the 11.44 tortious hours of driving or $25K? Her attorney will threaten that the judge will absolutely, unequivocally, without question or hesitation, cross-his-heart-and-hope-to-die, make your husband pay or participate in transporting the kids for visits. And there's a reasonable chance your husband's attorney will also "advise" your husband to accept some responsibility for transporting the kids, with both attorneys nodding their heads in solidarity at their understanding of how a judge will rule.

But here's the thing. And this is a biggun' so pay attention. <u>They don't know shit</u>.

Attorneys no more have an idea what a judge would rule than they can guarantee the ex will follow the Agreed Order that cost your husband $5,000 to obtain and of which the ex was a primary architect of the agreement. An attorney's goal, therefore, is to resolve matters *before* it gets before a judge *precisely* because it is a crap shoot for their client.

This means your husband cannot be worse off going before the judge. If the issue to be resolved is the transporting of the kids for visits, here are the following options for a judge:

1. Ex provides and pays for all transportation
2. Ex and your husband share the costs or drive time
3. Your husband pays/provides all transportation

The available outcomes (rulings) aren't exclusive to your husband. For your husband to continue to see his kids when they've been moved away, these are the *only* options at the **start** of the dispute. This means the ex has a 1 in 3 chance of a judge putting the transportation burden completely on her. And she and her attorney know this so they're going to pull out all the stops to get your husband to agree to option #3 and, if all else fails, settle for #2.

And this is where your husband has leverage – a lot of it – as he is in no worse position with a judge's ruling than he is negotiating outside the courtroom. So, tell him to dig in his heels until he gets what he wants; namely, none or so little of his time and money spent as to make the ex's decision to move painful only to her.

After the dust settles on this one, let's assume the ex either agrees to provide and pay for transporting the kids or a judge issues an order. What you may learn is that once the ink dries on that agreement/order (or is in the process of drying), the ex exclaims it is too far, too expensive, the kids have other things to do, other people to spend time with, it's inconvenient, the boyfriend's coming to town and she's certain the kids want him instead of dad, it's grandparents day and the kids "need" to spend time with the stepfather's parents ... a litany of excuses that all mean the same thing: she is refusing to abide by the agreement/order.

This leaves your husband with three options: 1) Give in and furnish the transportation because he really does want to continue being a father, 2) File a motion in the court for contempt, or 3) See the children infrequently or not again.

Not a single desirable outcome and all because the ex entered into an agreement she had zero intention of fulfilling. This is not to suggest your husband do nothing, especially when he actually wants to be part of his children's lives. I know moms who moved their children hundreds of miles from dad, refused to abide by the order requiring her to transport the kids to dad and then, when the kids started having problems in school, chastised dad for having less involvement. Moving kids away from another parent is an entirely sucky situation, hence my argument that courts should geographically shackle parents to each other until the kid is an adult. However, in the absence of logic and compassion for children in our courts, this is what people get. Especially when statistics bear out the effects of fatherless children. And they want to pin this crisis on dad?

While I believe my advice here is sound, this also intends to expose the things that can and do happen frequently with families who are more mobile today to better prepare you and your husband should the ex utter those fateful two words: "We're moving." It's then about getting a game plan together to minimize, first, the impact to the kid, and, second, the impact to you and your husband.

Create a move-away/visitation order that makes sense and imposes consequences.

It's important to understand that when it comes to the creation of mutually agreed upon visitation or move-away agreements, there isn't boilerplate language that lawyers or judges are to follow. That's right. Pretty much *anything*, absent something really unconscionable (e.g., denying visitation altogether for no reason), can be agreed upon by the parents. What you typically will never see in a visitation or move-away order is stuff like: *If the mother does not deliver the children for visitation as agreed, at father's discretion, he may transport the children, with any costs incurred by the father to be deducted from the monthly child support the father pays to the mother.* Or, *if mother fails to deliver the children to father for three (3) visits, in accordance with this agreement, absent any health-related condition, as supported by a physician's report, or other condition, as agreed upon by the parties, physical custody shall immediately revert to father with mother required to pay father $X in child support, with the following revised shared custody schedule.*

Here's the kicker: There is absolutely no reason why language like this cannot be included. Check with a lawyer if you don't believe me.

The beauty of spelling out financial or other consequences in an order is that the ex's restitution is then completely within your *husband's* control. Your husband doesn't need to return to court to request punishment for the ex for her refusing to comply with the court order. It's simple: She doesn't send the kids, he doesn't send her money. She violates the order enough times, kids are with him and she has to pay child support. It's a great incentive for the ex to follow an order.

Of course, when your husband proposes these consequences, the ex and her attorney will object. The bigger question your husband or his attorney should then ask them is: *Why?* If her intention is to abide by the agreement, why worry about repercussions for failure to abide? What situations could possibly exist that would ever justify the ex's failure to deliver the kid to dad per the agreement? If she's still balking, perhaps a discussion with the judge is then necessary as it certainly sounds as though her *real* intention is to blow off the visitation order. Under this line of questioning from your attorney in front of a judge, how might she explain her reticence? After all, the order even allows her an out for medical or mutually agreed upon reasons.

While attorneys may want you to believe it is not the Wild West in family court and that there are lots of restrictions on what parents can/cannot agree to, know that it is complete and utter bullshit. Black and white, unambiguous language (like, you know, in a *contract*) gives your husband a lot more leverage if having to enforce an order. (See or revisit Chapters Two and Three if you didn't get enough on lawyers and the courts.)

The ex agrees to transport the kids at her expense. It's simple, direct and unambiguous. Tough shit for her if, after she moves, she realizes she will actually have to spend her time and/or her money fulfilling her agreement. If she was too stupid to realize that at the time of making the agreement, then your husband dodged a bullet. If the ex is not stupid, then the ex is just ignoring the agreement and, essentially, telling your husband, kids and the court to go ... how shall I put it? Oh yeah. Pound sand. What? You thought I trot out the potty mouth for every occasion?

Keep an accurate count of the kid's overnights with dad.

Many states base child support on the number of overnights kids have with each parent. This means the parent receiving child support is entitled to more child support from the other parent if, for example, the children aren't with the other parent the minimum amount of time (e.g., every other weekend, once during the week, etc.), that serves as that state's basis for child support. Time is an important factor in establishing child support so it's wise to calculate the amount of time the kids are with your husband.

You might be surprised by how often the kids really are with their dad, especially if the child support amount paints a different picture.

All those times the ex asked your husband to keep the kids outside of the regularly scheduled visitation, and he happily obliged, adds up. Where states allow a child-support-receiving parent to squeeze out a few more bucks from the other parent for each additional overnight they can claim, know the challenge for the ex in the post-divorce dance is to remain vigilant in the kid being with her *on paper* more than they are with dad. Where this becomes problematic is when the ex has other priorities, she can't let dad know how much the kid is overnight with others and she's running out of babysitters. The ex may have no choice but to send the kiddies packing to daddy.

You may find the occasional extra weekday night stayover now extends to a week or more to accommodate the ex's work travel, a vacation or three with a new boyfriend or her honeymoons, all outside the visitation schedule. Consider that a $100 per month differential, in either direction, over a 15-year child support obligation, can amount to a whopping $18,000. That's an additional $18,000 the ex could receive (for the aforementioned vacations/honeymoons?) while you and your husband double-support the kid.

Could you use an extra 18 grand? Yeah, that's what I thought.

Let's examine this closer, shall we? Say the ex can't wait to go with her boyfriend to Hawaii for one week until the kid's Spring Break, when the kid is scheduled, per the court order, to be with her. Your husband happily agrees to take the kid for the additional week. Throughout the year, you're finding the kid is staying over, minimally, one additional night every other week. The ex also needs to take a couple of business trips where the kid stays over with dad another few nights. It's all cool.

It's also an additional 37 days per year, more than one month, or an additional 10% of the year (365/37 = 10.1%). Add that to a typical visitation schedule of 150+ days that includes summer break, alternating weekends, one night per week and miscellaneous holidays, and you're looking at 193 days per year or 53% of the year the kid is overnight with dad. (At 53%, it looks like a change of custody, doesn't it?)

The typical rebuttal from an ex whose kid is everywhere except at their house is that they still must maintain the household; even when the kid is spending an additional 10% of overnights with dad. (Hmm. Can't dad make the reverse argument?) Understand that child support also includes other expenses the kids can incur when with mom such as additional utilities, activities and food, expenses the ex <u>does not</u> incur when the children are not with her. So, let's say the ex receives $1,000 per month in child support. If the kid is with dad 10% above the court ordered schedule, and of which they based child support, the ex saves $100 per month or $1,200 per year when not feeding, bathing, heating, cooling or shuttling the kid. So, what hardship can the ex possibly claim were there to be a reduction?

If you find the kid is with your husband far more than what the child support award is based upon, urge your husband to keep a calendar of the time the kid is with him. If the increased number of overnights show a change of custody or would result in a reduction in child support in your jurisdiction, and there hasn't been any other substantial change in circumstances on your end – like your husband's big, fat raise that would prompt the ex to request an increase in support – ask him how *he'd* prefer to spend his savings?

That might wake him up.

CHAPTER SEVEN

When Stepkids Misbehave

If you have ever watched Judge Judy try a case involving a stepparent and a bio-parent, you will often hear her tell the stepparent that whatever is going on with the stepkid is not the stepparent's business, a stepparent is persona non gratis, and needs to butt out. Gosh, I would love to agree with Dame Judy but sometimes it's a little difficult to do when your unlicensed stepkid takes *your* car joyriding, holds an unauthorized party in *your* house that destroys *your* furniture, or steals *your* credit card. While I appreciate the Judge's position to a certain extent, situations that involve your stuff can certainly test your patience.

Regardless of the mayhem a stepkid may wrought, I firmly believe that when kids, step or not, repeatedly act out, short of there being some chemical imbalance, it is usually because their parent(s) or other relatives trained them to believe that crazy, illegal or illicit behavior gets rewarded. That's right. Some parents, grandparents, aunts, uncles, etc., in their zeal to win over a kid, will make excuses for the kid's misbehavior (this is a favorite for many insecure parents/relatives) or shower them with adulation and gifts whenever they roll a car, injuring people and property, disrespect others, fail school, sleep around, get busted for … you name it.

To give you an idea of how parental incompetence starts a kid on this path, consider a six-year-old testing his father's patience during his weekend visit with dad. After misbehaving throughout the day, the dad takes away the kid's Gameboy for one week. Upon returning the boy to his mom's, dad informs mom of the punishment and asks her to support the discipline. As the ex lovingly cuddles her son in her arms, she says to dad, "It doesn't matter. He doesn't play with it during the week anyway."

So that we understand what occurred: dad punishes child, mom dismisses dad's punishment in front of child, child receives warm, loving attention from mom. Kid's translation: Dad is an asshole. Mom is wonderful. I've done nothing wrong.

Yeah, that kind of stuff really builds a kid's character. And a tremendous amount of respect for dad to boot. This is going to turn out well for the kid.

When kids are young, their infractions typically include fighting with siblings, keeping a messy room and refusing to eat vegetables – not exactly stuff that would drive a parent or stepmom over the edge. If you have your own kids, you likely already understand these acts are routine, but consistent enforcement of rules usually corrects any wayward behavior. However, a parent, grandparent or other blood relative that allows a kid to get away with every transgression or makes excuses for the kid will most likely produce a difficult and behaviorally challenged child. Where mom and dad were once on the same page about the kids picking up after themselves, homework, curfews, and showing respect, in a contentious post-divorce setting, it may become like Disneyland at one or both parents' houses where it is now only all about having fun.

A friend with divorced parents recalled the time as a teenager she actively played one parent against the other. If her mom didn't give in to what she wanted, she would move in with dad. If dad started clamping down, she'd be back at mom's. She knew exactly what she was doing. Then, one day, one of the parents said: Enough. If you go to the other parent's house, you are not coming back. Today, she is a lovely, successful woman with a successful daughter of her own.

Unfortunately, all kids don't turn out that way. Too often, kids who grow up in dysfunctional environments can't shake off the craziness to become successful adults. The difficulty for stepparents when the stepkids' parents do a shitty job of raising them, lies in you wanting to correct the situation, especially when it creates turmoil in your house or influences your kids. It may be your kids will start to act out if they see you and your husband turning a blind eye to their stepsiblings behaving like idiots. It's hard to tell how this "blended" family dynamic will play out. Perhaps it's why Dr. Laura Schlessinger stresses that divorced parents not remarry until the kids are adults. I have certainly had my moments where I saw the wisdom in this advice.

But, if you're hell bent on marrying a guy with kids, the following tips may be helpful if having to deal with stepkids who may be less than stellar citizens.

Don't go out of your way for a misbehaving stepkid.

I know this sounds kind of harsh but, believe me, this will be one thing you can do that can keep you out of everyone's line of fire when – and trust that with a misbehaving stepkid it is a matter of *when*, not *if* – the kid misbehaves around you.

I believe a misbehaving kid was taught there are benefits to misbehaving; otherwise, why misbehave? I mean, if you got punished every time you stepped out of line, you might not step out of line. Call me crazy. So, it makes sense that if a kid continually misbehaves it is because someone is rewarding their misbehavior.

It's no big surprise. There are some parents out there who will give cars, trips, money and other goodies to a jail-bound kid who can't even be bothered to remember parents' birthdays or return their calls or texts – yet the good times, on their parents' dime, keep coming. Like the song goes, they are conditioned to receive. If they have no problem treating their own flesh-and-blood parents like garbage, imagine where you rank.

A twenty-something stepkid who struggled with school, honesty, alcohol, theft, fighting and frequent estrangements from family, accepted his stepmom's offer of a plane ticket for a long weekend as a surprise for her husband's birthday. Instead of accepting the offer as-is, stepson asked to stay longer than the weekend. Sure, why not? But we can't just leave it at that so stepson calls a few days later asking for his girlfriend to come along. Not this time, stepmom said, because of the plans she made for him and his dad. Stepson understands – until arriving the following month, girlfriend in tow (though staying with nearby relatives until getting the all-clear from her boyfriend).

Can she stay with us? stepson then asks. Dad, hungry for his difficult son's love, agrees to the son and girlfriend derailing stepmom's plans without discussing with her. Yeah, this goes over well for dad. So, now dad has to tell son it's a no-go with the girlfriend staying over but perhaps she can join them for dinner one evening.

I guess not as the following morning, stepson slipped out of dad's house without a word and did not speak to dad or stepmom for four years. Yes, four *years*. And lest you think the girlfriend was the love of stepkid's life, married and lived happily ever after, guess again. Two months later, the girlfriend got knocked up – by another guy.

But if you think that's pretty crappy …

When stepmom's in-laws heard of the hullabaloo, an aunt rushed to stepkid's defense, slamming stepmom for being a control freak, grandma suggesting to stepmom that she could have made arrangements to accommodate girlfriend, and stepson's mom took him on an all-expense paid trip to the Caribbean.

This is what I'm talking about. Unless your stepkids were raised by wolves, they learned that if they behave badly they receive rewards. Press a lever, get a pellet. I mean, come on, you disrespect your father, take an expensive airline ticket from your stepmother, trash them both to other relatives when you don't get your way and the payoff is lounging on a tropical beach, courtesy of mom? Where did *my* parents go wrong? I used to get slapped if I even thought a disrespectful thought. Any sand in my scenario would have been the stuff on top of my burial site for being an insolent, spoiled brat. It is as though some relatives are so afraid the kid will reject *them* – as they've witnessed the kid do to others – they will do whatever is necessary to avoid being cut off by the kid.

The important thing about this particular tip for the stepmom is if you go out of your way for a misbehaving stepkid in the hopes of creating a stronger relationship, because an obstinate stepkid has no motivation for engaging in healthy relationships, when things go south, as they will, it will be entirely *your* fault. Everyone, except your husband, will blame you for having created a situation that begged your stepkid's misbehavior, because had you not gone out of your way for the stepkid in the first place, there would not have been an opportunity for your stepkid to be a shithead; so, clearly, it's *your* fault.

Of course, it's faulty logic but goes back to you being an interloper, the outsider. You cannot expect the tribe to hold out one of their own and admonish them for bad behavior when there's a scapegoat in their midst.

That ain't gonna' happen. So, if you have a stepkid who is behaving like an asshole, don't lift a finger. Trust me, they have enough "real" family members who love to enable.

If the stepkids are failing school, there's nothing you can do. Really.

Kids typically have two parents with the ability to promote their kid's proper development, educationally and otherwise. If their parents choose counterproductive routes, such as refusing to cooperate with one another or stopping to date long enough to pay attention to their kid, your helping them with their schoolwork could produce the opposite effect, that of them resenting *you* for hassling them about their schoolwork. I mean, if the parents aren't on the kid's back about school and you, the interloper are, and since parents know best for their kids, obviously there is something wrong with *you*. Refer to the previous tip.

There is one caveat: Some kids may be downright starving for adult attention. However, you will know who they are and they aren't the ones misbehaving and they will most certainly welcome your help, in which case, help them.

Despite what I caution here, you may rationalize that a kid without education will eventually become a burden to you and your husband if the kid can't function in society. I've heard this one a lot from stepparents so they pull out all the stops (while, typically, the kid's parents sit on their ass doing nothing) to help the kid in the hopes they will one day be able to support themselves. This is a tough one because after years of neglect, and with adulthood looming, only then do the bio-parents become concerned their kid will make babies they cannot afford to feed ... with a high probability of a drain of cash from your household to their kid's household to stave off the babies' impending starvation. That's when they get their ole' behind into action.

One laughable example of this involved a divorced mom who had paid little attention to her children throughout their early school career. By high school, the kids each had 1.1 GPAs. It's been awhile, but if memory serves me, that's like massive failure. By her third marriage to someone wealthy and prominent, times had changed and in her social circle, other parents were busy preparing to send their kids off to universities around the country. The only problem for this mom was the very real possibility of her kids failing *high school*, much less getting into college.

But how do you keep up the façade of a devoted and caring mother with a successful family when the stink of failure is upon you? Allow me to tell you, dear. You take the kids on college tours. To other states. Just like your friends.

That's right. You book airline flights and hotels and drag the kids to schools where in all likelihood, they may suggest psychological help for the parent if even thinking of having the doomed student apply. Nonetheless, you scour the land, far and wide, for a school, any school, that will accept your disinterested, underachieving child so at cocktail parties you can toss out that little Jimmy and Susie are having amazing success at the University of We-Don't-Give-A-Shit-Who-Attends-As-Long-As-You-Pay-Tuition or, as contemporary news shows us, whichever school accepts bribes. Or, as oft happens in this circumstance – send them to a community college next door to the University that wouldn't accept them. Close enough.

My point is that if your stepkid struggles in school and you can clearly see their parents aren't joining forces to rectify the situation, long before other babies are on the scene, this could tax your resources to support the stepkid and their kids; not to mention the anger and resentment *your* kids might have at watching you take from them to clean up someone else's mess.

So, have a stern chat with hubby. Lay out the facts of life for him and if he isn't interested in a resolution now, you can't say you weren't warned. Then it becomes your choice how you want to handle things – especially if the kid and their kid are now living in your house and watching your HBO.

Above all, know this: If a kid is not motivated to obtain an education and their parents won't take the necessary corrective steps to ensure their children are on the right path, seriously, what are you gonna' do?

Don't expect to be remembered on any of your special occasions.

I know a stepmom who, along with her husband, vacationed with the stepkids in Europe, Mexico and the Caribbean. They bought the kids cars, TVs, video games, nice clothing and took them out to great restaurants.

The stepmom baked intricate birthday cakes for the kids, threw parties for them, spent hours working on Halloween costumes and always looked for interesting things to do when the kids visited their father. She can probably count on one hand the number of times the stepkids, after becoming adults, remembered her on birthdays or other special occasions.

This is a particularly thorny issue because after all you do/did for them and you get nuthin', it's like ... what the hell?

This is something else we can trace back to early education by the parents. In one family, when it was one child's birthday, the birthday child and their sibling (not a twin!) were both given gifts by family members. This went on for years. In fact, one child once said to me, "I got X for (my sibling's) birthday!" At Christmas, neither child was expected to think of their sibling; they were, as previously mentioned, taught only to receive. I think you can see where this is going.

But while you may be feeling unappreciated as yet another birthday passes and not even a two-word text comes your way, there may be comfort in knowing THEY ARE DOING IT TO EVERYONE THEY KNOW. That's right. Except for people they have sex with, they aren't doing shit for anyone, including mom, dad, siblings, grandmas, grandpas, aunts or uncles. And yet the good times, for them, continue.

Why? you might ask. Really? You need to ponder this? Straight out of the womb they're taught it is only good to receive. Nothing is reciprocal. They are the center of the universe and the purpose for the rest of you is to give, give, give to them. And here's the crazy part – the givers really do resent the shit out of the kid for being such a greedy taker yet they continue to give. Now, that's the definition of insanity.

For you, dear girl, don't do what the blood relatives of this kid do by trying to buy their affection in the hope they will 1) Not cut you off as they are apt to do or 2) Reciprocate with a Happy Birthday or Merry Christmas. If your stepkid is a selfish, self-centered jerk, no matter how much you do or have done for them, don't believe this entitles you to a space on their calendar for well wishes, much less being on their radar. You, like the others, simply aren't that important to them – until it is time for you to give, of course.

So, that leads you back to Chapter One, right?

CHAPTER EIGHT
Dad's Relationship with the Kids

Quick. Think of any relationship you have or had. It doesn't matter if it is/was good, bad, neutral. It just has to be between you and another human; so, no slipping in your favorite pet where it was a 24/7 unconditional lovefest or that one-night stand on that business trip to El Paso. I'm talking you, another human, and some serious time interacting. If it's with a parent, even better.

Now, think of any bumps in the road or, complete collapse, in that relationship. Maybe you struggle to have a meeting of the minds. Perhaps the other person is a challenge to be around. Maybe it's one of those love-hate things. You know, as in, "She's my mother and I love her but she's just so damn infuriating when she does X!"

I get it. I, too, have human relationships. Some good, some bad and some neutral. And most require a continual navigation of the relationship waterways. Every day, people maneuver through a labyrinth of their relationships and emotions, thinking such thoughts as: *Will she be upset if I tell her she needs to stop being such a bitch? Why the hell do I have to do all the laundry while he's just sitting there watching TV? If his mother comes over here one more time, unannounced, I swear I will lose it!*

Yep. Those are *our* relationships. Those are *our* feelings. We are the creators of *our* relationships. And we are responsible for managing these relationships. A friend may piss you off by treating you as her personal servant, but for them to even have a place to behave this way, *you* must give them space in your life. That means you have a giant hand in whatever your relationship is and when you have a giant hand in it, how it pans out is minimally 50% your responsibility. And that goes for any relationship. As I oft heard said before, you teach people how to treat you.

Now, about your fiancé/husband's relationship with his kid. Guess what? Whatever the relationship is, your fiancé/husband helped shape it. That's right. He gets to take at least 50% responsibility for the state of the relationship. And, early in the relationship, like at birth, he gets to take 100% responsibility. A baby can only do so much, right?

I can hear the chorus now – "*Even if…?*" Yes, *even if* the ex lies about your husband to the kids and they see your husband as the creep your ex tells them you are or the ex frustrates custody exchanges to the point your husband says, "*Screw this shit. My time is better spent knocking myself in the head than repeatedly going to pick up kids who aren't where they're supposed to be,*" or the ex refuses to provide your husband with any information about the kids' school and other events so that when little Jimmy receives his 10th award for being the smartest kid on the planet and his dad is conspicuously absent at the ceremony – for the 10th year in a row – because it "slipped" the ex's mind to tell your husband or the ex lured your husband to Iran just to "visit," stole his passport, and threatened he'd never see the child again if he runs away, requiring him to steal away in the night with the kid to Turkey (are you getting the *Not Without Daughter* reference?). Still 50% responsible.

How? you might ask. Simple. He chose the ex as the vessel to plant his seed to ensure his genes live on. As Dr. Phil says, "You choose the behavior, you choose the consequences.". In this case, he chose the field to plant and he's stuck with whatever it grows. After all, the ex didn't make him marry her and have kids so that whatever flows from your husband's decisions, it is now his responsibility to manage all ensuing relationships. Even if …

But, as I promised at the outset, this book is about you, baby, and how to keep *your* sanity intact. Your fiancé/husband's relationships with his kids is his business alone and like you, he should manage them. If the relationships are not good, would you prefer they be better? Of course. Who wouldn't? Where it becomes frustrating is when we, the outsider, the interloper, know exactly what everyone should do, say and how they should act to foster strong and supportive relationships but, sadly, our advice, mostly, falls on deaf ears. You are certainly welcome to give it the old college try – with your husband only – to enhance or repair his relationship with his children, should that be necessary, but if nothin' happens, ain't nothin' you can do.

I can't conceive why a kid would create an estrangement from a parent who has done nothing bad to the kid. Under those circumstances, if they do, it is most likely (ok, incredibly, highly probable) the kid (now, adult) is operating from (mis)information they received in childhood about that parent. If that statement I just made is untrue and the kid disconnects from a parent, *sans raison,* then the adult child is just fucking crazy. Hey, people don't just sever relationships with a parent, willy-nilly, without any foundation. There is always a reason. Unless, and I repeat, the kid ain't right in the head. And that's a whole different ball of wax.

Nevertheless, it never ceases to amaze when parents are so short-sighted when lying about the other parent to little kids who believe everything adults tell them. If a parent lies to their kid by telling them dad doesn't send enough money for them to eat, from a kid's viewpoint, dad is then a real shithead. Add to that the kid then going off to be with dad and seeing dad has just spent a boatload of money on a boat but, according to mom, they haven't enough money to buy food and *OMG, we're gonna' starve and it's that selfish prick's fault. I hate his guts!* This shit sticks with kids and when they're old enough to stop returning dear old dad's phone calls, they pull the plug. Or, is it, cut the cord? Though phones don't typically have cords that much anymore. You get the idea. They are hasta la vista, baby.

Situations like these suck big time. But, again, because this book is for you, dear, here are some handy, dandy tips to help you manage your emotions, tamp down frustrations and absolve yourself of any responsibility you may now or in the future feel is yours when it comes to your husband's relationship with his kid and miscellaneous others. Because it isn't your responsibility. Unless, of course, you're a troublemaker and like to get in other people's business, in which case, shame on you and your ass deserves a good kicking from the people whose lives you are meddling. If this is not you – and you wouldn't have plunked down your hard-earned dough for this book if you enjoy drama – then I hope the following tips will put you in a Zen state of mind. Ommmmmh.

Stay out of them (relationships, that is).

Are you getting the recurring theme?

Just imagine. Prior to you, your husband managed his kids, ex, family, friends and, if things were a bit contentious with the ex, an attorney or two. And he did this completely unassisted. Funny, though, how post-you, he is a gigantic heap of incompetency. I wonder why. Not.

I have a theory. And one that may make you feel better about leaving your husband to manage his relationships ... by himself.

First, I want you to consider how you might feel about going through a prickly divorce, halving your time with your children, giving up your home, losing half or more of your belongings, supporting your household and a fraction of a second household – on the same income! – and dealing with an ex who treats court-ordered visitation as only a suggestion. The pressure is mounting. People are becoming unreasonable. The kids hate shuttling between two homes and start acting out. The ex files another lawsuit to see if there is more money to be had from you. Your parents aid the ex in violating court orders by concealing the kids from you (Lawd only knows the reasons!) and your so-called friends are only too happy to report your ex's dating exploits.

I can see the sweat starting to bead on your forehead.

Now, imagine an unencumbered person comes along. Light, airy, fun, employed and without a single dependent. Instead of paying, minimally, 1.3x what others pay to live, your personal expenses are now 50% of what they were previously. Feelin' pretty good, right? To top it off, the encumbered person, delighted to be part of this new family, is equally delighted to manage your relationships with your children, attorney, and, if need be, your ex when causing problems with custody exchanges or creates sundry other annoyances. Giant sigh of relief, right?

So, the question isn't *why* would hubby relinquish control of his relationships? It's why *wouldn't* he? Seriously. It's not that big of a stretch.

Here's someone who's had a 20-ton weight dropped on him. You come along with a lever large enough to lift that weight. As he's lying there, splat beneath the massive weight, gasping for breath, trust he will not say, "I'm OK, honey. I don't need your help. I can manage all these people myself." Yeah. That won't happen.

As painful as it may feel, you need to resist the urge to lift that weight.

Here's a classic example of why: My youngest stepson had a car accident in his very first car and only had liability insurance. We had previously advised him to put half his earnings from his afterschool job into savings and have fun with the rest. Apparently, our suggestion wasn't as fun as having fun with *all* his earnings. Absent collision insurance to pay for the loss of the car and no money to replace the car, now, no car. What to do?

For a few weeks, he was aimless, bumming rides or borrowing my car. As much as it was a pain in the ass for me and my husband, we resisted bailing him out of his problem because: 1) It was *his* problem and 2) If he learned to solve this problem himself, he likely wouldn't get himself back into this mess. I won't bore you with the details of what happened next, like his buying a cheapo car for a few bucks, it breaking down, getting towed to a rip-off artist's garage, my nearly getting punched out by an illiterate mechanic, the sheriff providing him escort to regain custody of his broken down car, but, in the end and on his own, he bought himself a nice little car. The point being, especially if I lost you at the details I swore I wasn't going to get into, is that if you leave someone to take care of their stuff, most of the time, they'll take care of their stuff. And, once they learn how, they don't need you to do it. Get it? Great. Now, go do something important.

Leave relationship fixing to those in the relationship.

If memory serves, wedding vows usually don't include: "I promise to love, honor, cherish and repair all your broken relationships." For those who disregard the previous tip, you must believe your marriage license confers exactly this responsibility. (If you scratch the surface on this one, you'll likely find a woman pegged as her family's fixer. But that's another therapy session.)

If you're one of *those*, you will no doubt be tempted to pick up that phone and admonish a kid for being disrespectful or hurtful to their dad, especially if seemingly for no reason. How dare they dismiss the man who taught them to ride a bike, tie their shoes, the perfect cast, waterski, give a proper handshake, respect women, put them through school and always bought them their favorite ice cream. We're not talking a monster here so it baffles when a kid goes radio silent or is simply dismissive of a parent. Absent mental illness, any deep-seated anger a kid has toward dad may be traced to their heads receiving a steady diet of garbage early on. If that's the case, why take it out on the kid?

In fact, why do anything? You have no power here (said Glinda, the Good Witch, to the Wicked Witch of the West. Come on, girls. Wizard of Oz. Duh.). And it's true. It's tough, if not impossible, to infuse reason into an unreasonable situation created by unreasonable people. I can't fathom the destructive ideas floating around in a kid's head without basis if from a foundation of lies. The crazy part, and why there must be one huge ass internal tug-o-war going on in the adult kid's head, is their *experience* with their father often doesn't align with lies they've been told.

On the one hand, you may have mom lying her ass off about what a horrible jerk dad is but, on the other, when the kid is with dad, it's … wonderful and nothing like what they've been told. But, a kid reckons, *mom wouldn't lie. There must be something sinister about dad I'm just not seeing. He really* must be *withholding money from me and mom. It's why mom said I can't have new shoes (but wait, didn't mom just buy herself another pair of shoes? – delete this thought; not congruent with I-hate-dad thoughts) and now she says there's a possibility I'll have to have subsidized school lunches. I can't wait until I'm old enough to cut off the bastard.*

We shouldn't be asking why kids from a divorced family more often than other kids, abuse drugs and alcohol, perform poorly in school, are more promiscuous or get in trouble with the law. Nope. It is more accurate to ask: *Why wouldn't they?* as some parents can be selfish assholes.

But back to you. You can't fix this. Depending upon how deep the fractures, it may even take a team of therapists to correct. Meanwhile, as you look for ways to bring together the troubled ones, and unsuccessfully I might add, what is the world missing because of this giant distraction? And, believe me, that's all it is. Because, and I shall repeat, **you cannot repair others' troubled relationships**.

Periodically, there are epiphanies. That may include you realizing your husband has, all along, the ability to make grand gestures to correct any issues that may exist in his relationships with his kid and others. He may tell you he feels powerless against the lie machine or that he can't keep his family from causing problems but that's only an illusion … or an excuse.

For example, did you know a court can change custody in the snap of a finger if it finds one parent is alienating the other parent? Is it easy to prove? I don't know. I guess it depends on the circumstances or severity of the alienation. I suspect it also takes a helluva' lot of documentation, hiring an attorney, a court appearance, time and money. However, if the ex is actively destroying a relationship between kid and dad, and dad can prove it, the ex could have hell to pay. The thing is, it's not impossible for your husband to fix many of the issues he may be experiencing. He just has to take action. It may come at a cost, but that doesn't mean it is the impossible feat he's been saying it is.

Still, not your problem. And neither are the issues your husband may have with others in his world. In effect, if you are powerless to mend relationships, why waste your time trying? If I hear you muttering to yourself that you'll feel guilty if you don't take some action to mend some screwed-up relationship of your husband's, I swear I'll throw up. Guilt is only for those who've done something bad. You didn't create the dynamics of his relationships, so what "bad" have you done? See how that works? If there's any guilt to be had, make sure it is properly directed.

And show your husband some respect. Perhaps he distances himself from someone in his family for a good reason.

You may be (ok, you will be) blamed for the bad relationship between dad and kid.

Where it is dysfunction-palooza with your husband's relationship with his kid, rest assured that all kinds of relatives will be whipping out a finger and aiming it straight at you. But, as the saying goes, when pointing a finger at someone, you have three coming back at you. Profound, right? However, in such situations, it ain't likely the finger-pointers will see how their ... er ... *involvement* has been a major contributor to straining the relationship between your husband and his kid. So, if they aren't responsible for a kid's disrespect toward or estrangement from their dad, by process of elimination, it must be YOU! Forget that you only met this bunch a few weeks or months ago and that it has taken them years to cultivate this shit storm. That's too logical, sweetheart. Dysfunction, by its nature, prohibits taking responsibility.

Still, it may happen that your husband grows too exhausted to keep up the fight to have a normal father-kid relationship. (Pay close attention here as this will blow your mind.) After years, or decades, of an ex screwing with visitation schedules, dragging your husband into court for every one of her life changes that, not so coincidentally, upsets the hell out of previously hard-fought and outrageously expensive court orders, and family members (her's and his) united in the ex's fight, against what, we do not know, and now has a surly, floundering kid, all messed up from mom's (court-sanctioned) changing of husbands/houses/schools, your husband, broken and beaten, like the kid, may fly the white flag in surrender. Whew! And you thought that when dads went MIA is was because they were just being selfish jerks.

Who can blame him when every attorney he hires to protect his **kid's** right to be with him, measures victory by how much money the attorney can wrangle from your husband? What? You didn't really believe attorneys are in family law because they want to do right by kids, did you? I'll concede there may be that rare attorney who isn't running their own agenda and gets that it would devastate a kid to be moved to another state, away from dad, and will actually do the work to stop an ex's self-centered plans. Where you find them, however, is anyone's guess.

What all this means is, despite whatever the ex, her family, your husband's family, and their friends have done to create such a hostile situation, they see *you* as being the cause of this mess. Of course, you aren't. Trouble was brewing long before you showed up, but because some people are just not good at accepting responsibility for what they do, and if your husband stands up to these bullies, that must mean ***you*** are the troublemaker. It is why you may hear the ex saying total crap like, "Before you came along, everything was fine."

Of course things were great, honey. Your marriage was intact. Kids were happy. Life couldn't have been more wonderful. Seriously? What idiot with a failed marriage and wasting child support on attorneys to get more child support would think their lives were perfecto until you showed up? Oh, right. An idiot. It's why there was an opening for you, my dear.

CHAPTER NINE

Inheritance: To Give or Not to Give. That is the Question.

Inheritance deserves its own chapter. Why? Because unlike the weekly or monthly dough your husband is morally and legally obligated to shell out to keep his kid alive, distribution of funds, post-mortem, in many circumstances, is usually at the discretion of the owner of said funds. That means, just 'cause someone be related, don't mean nothin'.

Inheritance can be a statement of how the departed felt about their relationships with others. Considering that some adult kids treat their parent(s) pretty shabbily, the kid's name appearing in the will may not be the slam dunk they hope. But, treat parents well and there's a good shot they'll be hearing the words, "And my priceless 19th Century piano goes to (insert name here)." Don't, and there could be a real nice surprise in store.

My grandparents changed their wills frequently, depending on which of their adult children pissed them off that week. Just when everyone thought their estate had been settled, more recent versions of their wills (yes, plural) would surface. That tact probably isn't the best plan as, years after their deaths and little recollection of who got what in 1986, yet another asset arose, with their last remaining daughter receiving the proceeds. A few months later, another, seemingly last will popped up – remarkable how that happened! – and that very same daughter had been carefully carved from its pages. Too bad. She already got the cash.

Still, there's this whole mixing of your and your husband's money in bank accounts, house(s) you bought together, that amazing painting you both fell in love with in Florence during your second honeymoon, and let's not forget the Christofle silver you both have been curating for decades that all falls under the category of stuff that can be had by stepkids. And let's not forget you may have your own little heirs to consider. Ah, the plot (and assets) thickens. Now you can see why there is a need for this topic to have its very own pages.

While inheritance may not become topical for you until many years into your marriage, for stepkids (or their mom) it may be top of mind, right after hearing dad utter your name for the first time, with a look in his eye that tells them everything will be different now. It may not even matter if the inheritance we're talking about is a rusty '55 Chevy or a Tuscan villa. In the minds of some stepkids, what should rightfully be theirs could possibly be *her's*. Sound the alarm!

Just look at that gold digger!

And I don't believe I am off base here with the emotions stepkids experience over inheritance. In fact, most research on stepkids and inheritance focuses on the kids' fear that dear old stepmom will make off with dad's assets and they'll be left empty handed. Perhaps because men are perceived as contributing more to the family financial coffers than their spouse, ergo, it's *his* property? Shrugging shoulders here. Funny, though, stepfathers seem to get a pass on this one for some reason; probably because of the same reason, I suppose. More shoulder shrugging.

I had my own discussions with my stepsons about inheritance and I believe their thoughts, at the time of our discussion, were typical of many stepkids, as witnessed by the plethora of comments in online forums and discussions on many a talk show. The reaction I refer to is their belief – and not necessarily in a negative way, but more matter of fact – that should their father precede stepmom in death, minimally, half of the couple's assets is instantly conveyed to dad's kids. I've heard this from young and older stepkids.

This reminds me of a couple of Judge Judy episodes. The first involved a 14-year-old boy suing his stepmother for half the furniture in her house after his father died. The second was a woman suing her stepfather for a 20-year-old truck after her mother's passing. In the first case, the 14-year-old boy's mother was assisting him with the suit (big surprise). In the second example, the woman believed her mother's divorce from her father was not valid so the subsequent marriage to stepdad was also invalid; if invalid, her mother's property (the truck) would, therefore, go to her. And she claimed all this without any evidence.

Pain makes people do crazy things. So, if you're thinking you don't have any assets worth putting into a will, you may want to reconsider.

Before I go further, as a violent reminder, I am not an attorney. You would be well-advised to talk with an attorney regarding your estate planning questions and do not take what I write here as legal advice as this is purely a *philosophical* discussion. Nothing more.

That written, here's an interesting tidbit I read: In almost all states, except California, stepfamilies are not considered "real" families so probate (inheritance) laws don't apply to stepchildren. So, let's say your husband kicks the bucket without a will after 20 years of marriage to you. Now, everything is yours, much to the stepkid's disbelief and dismay. Then comes your turn to say adios. You, too, do not leave a will. Stepkid moves into position to take it all. Not so fast!

If your state does not recognize a stepkid as "family," they are then not entitled to inherit anything absent their inclusion in a will. Why would they, legally speaking? In the eyes of the court, they're strangers to you. Even if the stepparent's estate consists of money and property left by the stepkid's father, your *blood* relatives get first crack at it – and vice versa if the shoe is on the other foot. So, if stepkids are nervous they may not receive an inheritance, they may have good reason.

For widowed stepmoms with wonderful stepchildren and assets, you may wish to include the stepkiddies in your will and, hopefully, all will be happy. However, if the stepkids haven't been all that nice to you, maybe they ignored you for years or the estate is only enough to ensure your survival, you might not be feeling so benevolent or, perhaps you want to hang onto your last remaining 80 bucks to … live. Even in these circumstances, your stepkid may think of you as a wretched, miserly, selfish beast.

Why? Because even if your stepkids haven't said ten words to you in ten years, they may fully expect to be named in *your* will because despite being a shit to you for a decade or more, they truly believe whatever you own was given to you by their daddy and your death is their chance to get it back. If the kid has been an ass for a long time, I promise it will all be too convenient for them to forget you worked your ass off your entire life to build a life and an estate with your husband.

In this case, your best offense is defense. Yeah, I know, I wrote earlier that defense is an act of war but when it comes to inheritance, depending on your personal circumstances, you'll likely want to take some preemptive steps to minimize as much angst as you can, while you can. As I promised, this book intends to reduce the crazy in *your* life.

Discuss how you and your husband will handle inheritance.

You may be young and are just now mixing assets or you may have been married for years and now have lots of them. You may have children of your own from a previous relationship or are childless but planning on having kids. Whatever your situation, discuss early on with your intended or hubby how you want things to play out in the event of your deaths; preferably, *before* marrying. And I'll tell you why.

If waiting until the ink dries on your marriage license to discuss who-gets-what, you may be surprised to learn your husband intends to leave it all to his kids who treat you as their personal maid or owe you both more money than the national debt. Your husband may tell you he feels he "owes" the kid because after his divorce he was blah, blah, blah, blah to the kid and a nice big, fat inheritance will make it all better. Of course, your husband will be dead at inheritance distribution time, so not sure how all will be "fine," but when it comes to someone else's kids, don't underestimate the power of guilt.

And what will happen should hubby exit too soon, leaving minor kids? If this isn't addressed in his will, a prior court order or he hasn't purchased life insurance exclusively for the support of his kids, *you* aren't legally obligated to support the kids or include them in a subsequent will. This could open one serious can of worms there, chickie.

In addition to his kids, you may also have your own. So, what if your husband has three kids and you have one? Do you divvy up your stuff four ways or do you split it down the middle, dividing your husband's share three ways and your kid gets your full half? What if one or more kids are jerks? Will you be turning over in your grave at the thought of a nasty stepkid dining on *your* Aunt Mildred's antique lace tablecloth? But wait! What if you and husband produce a joint heir?

There are a myriad number of ways to assign inheritance to kids or others with each avenue a potential minefield. If your husband goes first, you may be tasked with this unpleasant duty, unless your stepkid has been a complete ass throughout your marriage, in which case you may look forward to the day they read *your* will. Even absent tumultuous family relationships, the issue of inheritance is, at best, tricky. Would-be recipients are shy to ask what you have in store for them as that might give off a greedy vibe.

When I talked with my stepsons about inheritance, I asked them about specific things they might want. There were a few standout items so that makes our estate planning easier. As to the logistics in them getting some of these things, unfortunately, we'll have to leave it to them as we'll be … let's say, indisposed.

One thing I hope to accomplish at the time of my departure from this earth, is that I don't leave anyone feeling unloved. That isn't always the case with others. In some instances, people use (denying) inheritance as their final F-U to those who they feel hurt or disappointed them in life. In other cases, I've witnessed how a seemingly, unfair inheritance can shred siblings' relationships, with brothers and sisters never to speak to one another again. Really? Over a car or a few (Ok, maybe a lot of) bucks?

I hope you can see the wisdom in discussing inheritance before you marry. Or, if you're already married, get things rolling. You never know when they'll be calling your number.

Dad needs to speak with his kids about inheritance.

Know that kids, yours or step, generally have no clue what your estate consists of unless your fiancé or husband is Donald Trump (and even that's a big question) or some other public figure. Typically, what most kids know about their parent's estate is what their eyes can see or what they've been told the parents own. They have no clue whose money, yours or your husband's, went into acquiring your stuff. And for those of you who take the whole we-are-one marriage thing as intended, who-paid-for-what is a non-issue – for you and your husband; though maybe not so much for the stepkids. In their minds, it's more like 50-50, even if it has been 90% you and 10% your husband. Because your husband is a man, they will more than likely believe, even if blatantly and obviously untrue, that he furnished the cash that made up the estate.

The point of your husband having a talk with his kids about your estate and inheritance plans is to advise or remind them that you and your husband are *married*, that being married means building a life together, spouses are to take care of each other, and that their assets, unless there is so much money it can't be spent by one person in their lifetime, may need to be earmarked for the surviving spouse's care.

They may not believe you two will last that long, as your husband has at least one divorce under his belt so that marriage, in general, may be viewed as a casual event, but it is worth a shot. Your husband can assure them that when the time comes, and should you be the last person standing, there's been a decent enough relationship, and there are remaining assets at the time of your passing, they shouldn't worry about not being included in your will – provided, of course, *you* aren't a bitch. I wouldn't think you are, especially since you're the one who bought a book on how to reduce the effects of the crazies around you.

Now, I chose the words "decent enough relationship" instead of "great" because even if it has only been a cordial relationship with your stepkid, including them in your will is the moral thing to do as their father did contribute some, if not all, the assets to the marriage. And do you really want to bid *adieu* knowing people will always talk shit about you? Personally, I hope when I am gone and someone thinks of me, stepkids included, it will bring a smile to their faces, as opposed to fantasizing about my second death. Yikes.

You're not obligated to leave your estate to nasty and abusive stepkids.

We live in an era where kids receive rewards simply because they exist. Children of divorce, especially when the divorce is acrimonious, carry the added bonus of parents vying for the kid's love by over-giving even when a situation warrants a swift kick in the ass versus a new Camaro. This ridiculous parenting style has created a generation of snowflakes whose only skill is receiving goodies regardless of how they behave.

Allow me to illustrate. A 13-year-old boy lived with his mom in a different state than his dad. Since the divorce, mom made little to no effort to raise the kid to consider, much less respect, his father. Court-ordered visitation with the dad was an *inconvenience* to the mom, fraught with repeated demands that dad and kid go without seeing one another if that week or weekend just didn't fit with her plans. Father's Day and Christmas, the kid routinely showed up empty-handed. A few years of this indoctrination and the kid came to view his dad as a wallet and not much more. And how much respect do people show cowhide?

One Spring Break, when the kid was to be with mom, in accordance with the court-ordered visitation schedule, instead, the boy was to travel with a friend and friend's father to the beach town where, coincidentally, his dad resided. When dad learned of the plan, he told his son that if he was not going to be with his mom for Spring Break, he was to be with him – not some other kid's father. Court ordered.

What happened? you ask.

One day, in advance of the scheduled trip, the dad received an extraordinarily well-crafted letter from (his middle school failing) son on his intention to keep his travel plans with his friend and friend's father, that dad has no say in the matter. Interesting. Especially the precisely written and grammatically correct letter. We might wonder how a kid with such exemplary writing skills was failing school. But I digress.

Put something like that to a guy who ensures your very survival and you can imagine how it turns out – for the kid. A quick call to the friend's kid's father puts an end to things very quickly ... for the kid.

Where is this going? you are asking again. I'll tell you.

Kids led by a parent or parents to believe that the kid calls the shots with grown-ups tend to become obstinate and disrespectful as they get older. Dad's telling you to shape up and start paying attention in school? *I'll show him who's boss. I'll get drunk and roll a car.* Yeah, that makes perfect sense. Nonetheless, a pattern is forming and, depending upon how much enablement goes on in the kid's family, the result can be one nasty, surly, disrespectful punk.

Do you want to turn over what you and your husband worked a lifetime to acquire to a little shit like this? It's something to ponder. But I also have a suggestion, one that shifts the responsibility to where it belongs. I got your back, girl.

Here it is: Have your husband discuss with his kid the ramifications of crappy behavior on their receiving inheritance. It's not unreasonable to explain to an older kid or adult kid how people who have worked hard to build an estate, even if the estate is a bicycle, may have mixed feelings about giving that asset to someone who treats them like garbage. Your husband can advise the kid that when making decisions about the future, it is the *present* determining those decisions. And the kid either gets it and adjusts or doesn't give a shit and proceeds business as usual. In which case ...

Don't feel guilty if you leave nothing to stepkids who don't shape up.

As I wrote earlier, guilt infers wrong-doing and if you have not done anything wrong to the stepkid but the stepkid has done nothing but wrong to you, why feel guilty?

Conversely, don't manufacture reasons to disinherit a stepkid.

Don't you just love it when a stepparent tells you they see their stepkid as their own – then drops them like a stone for some perceived slight?

Let's not forget that divorce is hard on kids and that they are at the mercy of their parents' post-divorce behavior. If one or both of their parents are vindictive and train the kids to hate the other parent, despise you, and allow them to behave however they choose, is it really the stepkid's fault they turn out to be assholes? I'm not so sure.

The "kid" may no longer be a kid and it would be a fair argument they can't blame their continuing obnoxious, rude, dismissive behavior as an adult on one or both parents. At the same time, there are some kids whose parent told them some pretty outlandish, but untrue, stuff about the other parent that the kid, later as an adult, continues to believe because they never confirmed its truth. They just go through their entire lives thinking and saying to whoever will listen, *Daddy's such an asshole.* Meanwhile, "Daddy" gets the cold shoulder from kids he worked his ass off to support, believing his kids are a bunch of ungrateful jerks. (At least, that's what I'd believe if I were him.) You really have to weigh the circumstances.

When it comes to inheritance, you need to put on your big girl panties because inheritance is a grown-up matter, not a tool to retaliate because an immature or emotionally destroyed stepkid hurt your feelings. If the kid's dad entrusted *his* estate to you – recall that half was his – a kid saying something mean to you or not seeing you anymore isn't reason to deny them their birthright. Think I'm wrong? Imagine you're the first to go, leaving behind your child from a previous relationship, and your husband decides your kid gets nothin' if for no other reason than your kid ain't hangin' with him anymore.

It's never comfortable when the shoe is on the other foot, right?

CHAPTER TEN

The Ex

Central to the crazy you are experiencing – if not, then why buy this book? – is ... da, da, da (ominous music, if you didn't get that) ... the dreaded *ex*. The mother of his children. The light in their children's eyes. Goddess Mom.

When we think of motherhood, as a concept, we often envision a Disney version – sweetness and light, baking cookies and cuddling with a bedtime story. What we don't expect is harassment, conniving, lying, selfishness and manipulation. It, therefore, comes as a giant surprise to many would-be stepmoms that the ex, a.k.a. mom, is, to put it gently, a raging bitch in Mary Poppins clothing.

When this realization hits, there is often a rush of emotions. In one moment, you might find yourself wondering how to cut someone's brake lines. In another, you're hoping that a friendly lunch invite to the ex will have you forge enough of a relationship for her to dial back the craziness a notch or two.

I get it. Believe me. I really, truly get it.

One thing I've learned about people is that they rarely, if ever, become someone else just because you want them to. Clichéd sayings, such as a leopard never changes it spots, exist because they're true. Short of some monumental, earth shattering event, e.g., prison, war, or atom bomb, people don't wake up one day and say to themselves, *I'm going to stop being such an asshole.*

Nope. If they've been traveling down the asshole path since childhood, they will continue. If they lie, cheat, steal and mistreat others, this is who they are. Maya Angelou said it best: *When people show you who they are, believe them.*

So, for your sanity, when it comes to the ex, whoever, whatever she is – be it a liar, manipulator, phony or scammer, know that is exactly who you're dealing with and, absent the aforementioned catastrophes, with 99.9% accuracy (for you know how scientific this book is, right?), will remain this way. But don't despair, little one. This is actually good news as it sets you free from any hope the ex will eventually become a decent human being.

And why is that good news, you ask? When you deal with what is and not as you want things to be, this puts you in the position of acting versus *reacting*. The ex is unreliable. OK. The next time she tells your husband she will deliver the kids to your house by 6 PM, when they pull into your driveway at 7:30 PM you will not explode as this is exactly what you expect from her. Your husband discovers the kid had an important school event that "slipped" the ex's mind to tell him? Rather than researching where to buy a battering ram to drive it through her house, accepting her deceitfulness will have you seek other ways to learn about important events for the kid.

When they forecast rain, we bring an umbrella. When we know flights are often late to depart, we bring stuff to occupy our time. We prepare for many other of life's inevitables, so why not also do the same with an ex who is equally predictable? That's right. If the ex is consistently problematic, that makes it so much easier for you to anticipate how she will behave so you can be proactive in how you act when she behaves exactly as you expect. Voila! No more blindsiding.

Don't do things in the hope it will set an example for the ex.

You and your husband alter your schedule eight weeks in a row to accommodate the ex's ever-changing visitation requests thinking she will reciprocate, yet the one time your husband needs to make a change, she will not accommodate. You wash and neatly pack the children's clothes for their return to their mom while she sends the kid with a mishmash of dirty clothes for their time at your house. You pack healthy lunches for the kids though she barely gets a cold hot dog into their lunch bag. You tighten your belt to pay for the stepkid's car or college tuition yet the ex does not but is never seen in the same outfit twice. You spend hours with the stepkid shopping for the right birthday gift for their mom, while the kid shows up at dad's for every one of his birthdays (much less, yours) without so much as a handmade card. You seethe, realizing the ex is self-centered, inconsiderate and selfish, but hope your selfless, compassionate and considerate ways will have her evaluate her own behavior to become a decent human being – just like you.

Are you nuts? That will never happen. If the hot dog queen conducts her life this way, no amount of you doing things the right way will ever change this. This is a mission that will never be successful so don't bother doing things with the sole aim the ex will learn by example. Do you need reminding? *When people show you who they are, believe them.*

Don't be surprised if she alludes that she and your husband are having an affair.

This might happen when you and your husband's ex are exchanging words (jabs). Just when you think you have the upper hand the ex insinuates that she and your husband are seeing one another or have had some clandestine "meeting."

Take a deep breath, dear girl. And then take another for this is a pure power play; unless, of course, you have real evidence she is telling the truth in which case, ditch this book and get the hell out of there. Seriously. But, if this is not true, then the ex is just stirring up the ole' insecurity. And, if your husband and the ex had been together for any length of time and your relationship with your husband is fairly young, the ex may have an edge as she likely knows your fiancé/husband better than you. So, yeah. That can make someone feel a little insecure.

However, don't buy into it. And don't attack your husband the second he walks through the door after such a conversation with the ex; unless you have hard evidence, of course, in which case, go to town on that lying, cheating piece of … Wait. I'm off the rails again. Back to the issue at hand. When an ex tosses a grenade at you, it's a diversion for you calling her out on some infraction. BUT – and I am so excited to tell you this – if you've been following these thousands of words in this book, <u>what the hell are you doing having a conversation with her in the first place</u>?

Should you not be able to avoid being at some kid-related event, outside of giving a cursory hello, what reason could possibly exist that puts you in a position where the ex can drop a bomb on you? As I write this, I can just hear the muttering in your head. *You see, I* had *to talk with her about little Jimmy's birthday party. I* had *to let her know I would be picking up little Susie from school because my husband couldn't. I* had *to tell her she can't keep calling my husband for nonsense things!* And the list goes on and on and still not a single, viable reason for you to engage in lengthy discourse with the ex. I mean, it's not like the two of you are friends. If you were, you probably wouldn't have felt the need to buy this book, right?

If we're to be honest here, girl (the truth shall set you free!), it's something more than just information sharing you use to justify talking with the ex. It's curiosity. I get it. This is a woman that the love of *your* life most likely once loved. And if she's a giant pain in the ass, you are really curious what is was about her your husband found so attractive; unless, of course, if she's gorgeous, in which case you may have your answer.

The funny thing is that she, too, is curious *and* worried about you. For starters, she's been replaced despite the hope her ex, your husband, would have just shriveled up and died when she left because she's so spectacular and he would be devastated by her leaving. Second, and probably most important, is that another woman, a mother-figure, is in a position to shape her children, comfort them when they are frightened, provide guidance as they navigate life and make memories unique to them.

Fear then supplants gratitude that her children have another person in their life who loves and cares for them. It's not a particularly happy place to be. It's why you may be experiencing so much thrashing about from the ex. If you're a previously divorced mom who has her own stepmom insecurities, you certainly get it. So, perhaps, a little slack may be due. That means, **<u>stop talking to her</u>**.

Sometimes you gotta' blow up the ex's plans to change behavior.

If you've been paying attention, you will have stayed out of or mitigated many potentially contentious issues with the ex. But try as you might, the ex may be hell bent on making sure your life is nothing short of, well, hell. You may deserve it if you had something to do with the demise of her marriage but if not, then there is no reason to be this woman's doormat or whipping post. Sometimes you just have to stand up for yourself but know that sometimes words are not enough to stop outrageous behavior. You may have to wait for that perfect moment to let the ex know just how much power you really do have.

For example, let's say your husband's ex isn't one to politely ask to change visitation dates or request help in other areas for the kids but, instead, demands and snaps her fingers as though your husband is still her husband – which, if that is how she operates, it may explain why he's *your* husband now. Let's say this goes on for months or years and you're exhausted by this woman running your lives. Now, let's say she finds another victim to marry, they've set a date, planned a Hawaiian honeymoon, and, once again, she demands that your husband drive 200 miles to pick up the kids, during the court-ordered time she is to have them, drive them back to your house and, upon her return a week later, your husband is to drive the kids 200 miles to return them to the ex's and then return home, another 200 miles. As discussed in Chapter Six, we're talking driving 800 miles over 10 hours so the not-so-nice ex may lounge, unfettered, on a tropical beach, sipping Mai Tai's with her new paramour.

The logical and most likely reaction would be for you to tell your husband to tell his ex to kiss your asses. The audacity! Right. Big fucking surprise. I don't think so. So, before you rant and rave a single moment, look at moments like these for what they are – golden opportunities to change her behavior. They are few and far between and you must keep your head about you if you're going to spot them when they're happening so you can make a better choice. And that better choice? Have your husband tell her, *Absolutely! We would love to take the little munchkins. I'm delighted to drive 800 miles.*

Unfortunately, for the ex, the day before she and subsequent hubby are to leave for their honeymoon, disaster strikes! Your husband can't pick-up the kids. However, if the ex can get the kids to and from him and then back to her, he'll gladly take them.

The beauty in this is that 1) It's a ***disaster*** – what can anyone expect in a disaster?, 2) How many people, at the last minute, are prepared to babysit kids who literally have nowhere to be for an extended period, e.g., school, that will allow a person to continue with their lives, e.g., work, and 3) The kids will have a wonderful time on their mother's honeymoon in Hawaii, where they may also discover that glass louver windows in the hotel room make a great ladder but, unfortunately, are not as strong as a real ladder but can be a lot more costly to replace than a ladder. It's win-win ... well, two out of three winners ain't bad.

The point I am making is that some stepmoms go out of their way to accommodate the ex's demands in the hope of keeping peace and having the kids feel happy and secure, knowing everyone is getting along, blah, blah, blah. But know this – not all exs care if their kids are happy, secure and everyone gets along. Some operate out of frustration, some feel entitled to do whatever they choose and some are just assholes.

Her relationship with your husband didn't work out. But their having children together does not give the ex license to beat the life out of you and your husband to get what she wants. Sometimes you just need to send the ex a big ole' message that you're not going to take her crap. And, if you think taking a step like the foregoing example is a defensive move, thus an act of war, nope. That is clearly an offensive move as the ex will probably not want to rely upon your husband again in a similar circumstance. Mission accomplished.

CHAPTER ELEVEN

More Really Important but Miscellaneous Challenges That Didn't Earn Their Own Chapter

Don't expect his kids to be happy their father is getting remarried.

You do realize the celebrities' blended families you see on TV or online don't always depict what's really going on in that family, right? Where so many "regular" folks struggle with abuse, neglect or just plain disinterest at the hands of a stepparent, it's inconceivable that celebrities, by virtue of celebrity-ness, have better odds at creating a happy blended family. Come on! Even the Kardashian-Jenners aren't immune to the blended family blues. Hell, it's sometimes challenging enough to deal with people with whom you share a bloodline, much less with a pack of unrelated strangers.

So, while you may not be able to contain your excitement at becoming a stepmom, I sincerely doubt the kid is equally, or is anywhere near the same vicinity, excited at becoming your *stepchild*. Think about it. Qualifying as a stepkid means your parents have split up, you shuttle between two homes, have two different lives, likely have to deal with kids you don't know or may not even like, have fewer resources available to you than had your parents stayed together and now you have to miss out on that science camp or school trip to China because your stepsister needs expensive therapy because *her* father is also remarried and is now devoting more time to his stepkids. Give me a moment. I'm out of breath on this one.

If you've been a stepmom who received pushback from the stepkids for any length of time, and have experienced issues following your marriage, you will most definitely understand what I'm talkin' about here. However, for newbies, it may come as a complete shock to learn the kids aren't as thrilled as you and their father about your impending marriage. 'Cause it just ain't so. And that's even if they kind of like you.

For younger kids, in particular, your marriage signals that their family will never reunite. Prior to my marriage, I dated a man with an 11-year-old daughter. She immediately took to me. We were like best girlfriends. In fact, I liked her a whole lot more than I liked my boyfriend. One day, the girl received word her mother was remarrying and became upset. I asked why and she said this meant her parents would never get back together.

I knew this little girl was very fond of me as I was of her. Her wanting her parents to get back together had zilch to do with me or even my relationship with her father. In her child eyes, one thing had nothing to do with the other. For other kids, however, if not for your existence, their parents may have a shot at reconciliation. Or so they think. That you are there, bigger than life, and dad is now all gaga over you, reconciling isn't possible. And, again, that's your fault. (You're getting the theme here, right?)

It would be nice to assure you that in time the stepkid will come around and forget their dream of an intact, biological family. But, I can't. For incredibly obvious reasons. This may explain why so many second marriages fail. Contentious relationships with soon-to-be stepkids, young and old, can put a lot of pressure on a new bride, especially since, as a woman, you likely want harmonious relationships, while kids, who don't share the same sentiment as you, may be searching for ways to sabotage the marriage. Hey, it can and does happen. Recall *The Parent Trap*? And that can go for new and established marriages which leads us to ...

If stepkids try to sabotage your marriage, have your husband handle it.

Kids are crafty little creatures and can be resourceful in getting what they want. If *The Parent Trap* isn't enough, then you'd be wise to watch *Yours, Mine and Ours* (the original – much more craftiness) with Lucille Ball and Henry Fonda, circa 1968. Even if the kiddies look like little angels and appear to be overly welcoming to you, don't be surprised if they lie about you to their father (if you're lucky, get you drunk – see the movie) or to their mother who's been aching to have a go at you.

If your husband becomes pissed off over the antics, let him handle it with his kids. You've got to understand that kids really don't like a lot of upheaval in their little lives. They want things to go back to what they were pre-you even if their parents' marriage wasn't great. But whatever you do, don't confront the kids. Aside from driving a big wedge into your relationship, this will give their mom more ammo for her cause.

If, however, your husband doesn't believe their little angel is capable of such subterfuge, refer back to Chapter Five. If you're already married and in the throes of sabotage, you will need to have a heart-to-heart talk with hubby to put a period to this kind of behavior if there is any hope of your marriage surviving. If you are in the planning stages of your marriage, better to get this out on the table now before you put down that deposit on the banquet hall because as I wrote in Chapter Five, a signature on a piece of paper, (marriage license) only changes things at the IRS.

And, of course, you can always wait to marry when the kids are up and out of the house and, hopefully, then it is a non-issue. Dr. Laura would be so proud of me for hauling out her advice here.

Don't expect and certainly don't force stepkids to call you mom.

You may be Mother Theresa while their own mother, eh, not so much. It doesn't matter. Regardless, you would be well advised to never, ever, under any circumstances ask, expect or force a stepkid to call you anything other than by your first name. If the kid has a mom, her name is "mom," and it doesn't matter if she is the worst mom on the planet. It is the rare child, young or older, who doesn't refer to their mother as "mom" even when her misdeeds are played out in the media.

Unless the ex has abandoned her kids or they know nothing about her, expecting or forcing a stepkid to call you mom is never a good idea. I can assure you that you will piss off the mom. And you know what happens when that happens, so it is safer for you to keep it on a first name basis only.

To give you an example, and although this story involves a stepfather, it is equally applicable to stepmoms. One stepfather, who after marrying a mother of two, demanded the stepkids call him "Dad" and to call their father by some other name. I know, crazy, huh? That didn't sit well with the kids so, guess what? They told their *Dad*, who then admonished the ex who was dismissive of dad's request by telling him to "grow up." Brilliant comeback considering the internal turmoil her kids were experiencing, wouldn't you say?

So, the kids took things into their own hands by not calling the stepfather anything – at all. If needing to communicate with the guy, the kids would ask their mom to relay their message. The stepfather eventually conceded to not being called "Dad" but because he didn't feel right being called by his first name, for some bizarre reason, he asked the kids to select a name of some inanimate object by which they could call him, something like, *Rocket*.

This also did not go over well with the kiddies.

Now, this stepdad is long gone (shocker, huh?) but makes for an amusing story; although, at the time, not so amusing for the kids. So, before you think it a great idea to force feed your stepkid the name, "mom", ask yourself if this is purely to satisfy your ego – the adult who has control over your life – or is it beneficial for the kids, who have no control except for resenting the shit out of you for forcing them to do things they are not comfortable doing.

You're better than this, girlfriend.

Don't badmouth the mother to or in front of your stepkids.

Unless, of course, you want to absolutely decimate your relationship with your stepkids. ***She's their mother, for crying out loud.*** Do you remember when someone said something nasty about one of *your* family members?

Even if you agree with them, you would still go to battle to protect their honor. Well, it's like that for the stepkid.

You may find the ex to be evil incarnate. She puts on a production for your husband's family that she's a loving and caring mother, all the while every word that comes out her mouth should receive Donald Trump-style fact-checking. She so kindly and generously remembers **your** mother-in-law at Christmas and her birthday while teaching the kids to blow off their dad on his birthday or Christmas. She hosts Father's Day parties for her boyfriends, complete with a gift of fluffy dog slippers for the new love, yet pointedly sends the kids to dad without even a card for Father's Day. With a chick like this, you not only fantasize about ratting out her wretched behavior to the kid, you want to take this news to the mountaintops where all the land, near and far, can hear. Barring that, you pray Karma is paying attention and she'll get her deserved comeuppance.

But whatever you do, keep it zipped. Kid's aren't stupid. Depending on their age they know when one parent is dishing dirt to the other. They hear their mom talk crap about you and your husband but, come on, she's *mom*. What are they going to do when they are just kids? Cut her off? Block her number on the cell phone? Seek Dr. Phil's help? None of these. They may, however, act out when they're with you and your husband if you bad mouth the old lady. They may steal your car, money and liquor. They may become disrespectful punks. It's about all the power kids have to demonstrate they don't appreciate you talkin' trash, even if deserved, about their mom.

I might interject here that a good rule of thumb with this is not at all dissimilar to the Golden Rule of do unto others as you would have them do unto you. You don't like others outside your family criticizing your family members? Guess what? Neither do the stepkids. It's not a complicated concept, dear.

You're not Chief of Morality P.D.

Kids have a different view of their mother than do you and your husband. Where you may think the mother is irresponsible for allowing the kids to blow off their homework in lieu of her taking them to the beach, to the kid, that makes mom cool. Conversely, your husband is the opposite of cool when making them do their homework. Where you believe the ex sets a bad example when shacking up with yet another guy on vacation, kid in tow, the kid sees it just as a vacation not that mom is an irresponsible and shameless slut. Consider, however, that you are not the morality police, they are not your kids, and no matter how questionable you find the ex's behavior (that will most likely mar the kids for life), it's none of your business or concern.

Your husband may see this differently. He may want his children to grow up to become decent, moral and law-abiding citizens. If the ex's behavior is so morally corrupt as to twist little minds, your husband can do something about it. But you don't need to.

Your fretting about how your stepkid will turn out when the ex believes it is harmless to play beer pong with her minor child and his friends and fleeing the crime scene when the police arrive will only make you crazy. If a parent sees nothing wrong with their aiding their child to break the law, know that your moral stance isn't on her radar. So, what's the point of killing off your brain cells? (You know that stress, especially chronic stress, kills off those puppies, right?) Honey, you have far better things to worry about. Besides, you don't have an ounce of power to fix this.

If this bothers your husband, let him screw with this. And the beat goes on.

Don't force your religion on the stepkids.

Your husband may happily go from Protestant to snake handling for you but please don't force stepkids to convert, or even participate, just because they happen to be with you on church day, unless they don't object. Though I might object to little ones coaxing rattlers from their slumber to prove a religious point.

Religion is an intensely family or personal decision, with the children's religion usually decided long before you showed up. I would certainly take offense to a different religious indoctrination going on with my children at the urging of my ex and his new bimbo. (What? I'm not telling you something you don't already know? In many an ex's house, bimbo is often the official name of the stepmom.) In fact, I'd be downright pissed off if

I learned a stranger was imposing her religious beliefs onto my children, and most especially if the views are diametrically opposed to my religion.

I don't mean to suggest my religion is better than another. Far be it. But the issue of which religion the kids should follow, until they can make their own decisions, can be difficult to reconcile as the children also belong to dad and dad may now have new religious views (courtesy of la bimbo). So, what if the ex and kids are practicing Catholics but dad's new wife is Jehovah Witness? How about Jewish and Mormon or Muslim and Greek Orthodox? Depending on the ex and his spouse's commitment to the religion, there will certainly be times for exposing the stepkids to the tenets of the other religion.

For you, however, the situation is easy-breezy-lemon-squeezy. Ask your husband to decide how he prefers to handle this should the stepkid be with you on your worship days. If taking the stepkid to temple instead of Sunday Mass creates a big brouhaha, just leave hubby at home with the kids while you do your own thing. I mean, really, if practicing a religion, any religion, intends to make us act more kindly to one another, why create trouble with the ex who in turn will retaliate and the dance is on …? Lest you've forgotten, this book is to reel back the angst, not create more of it. Aren't you glad I'm keeping you focused and on track? You're welcome.

Accept that the stepkids live in two different worlds so don't penalize them when they get things wrong.

Even after my youngest stepson lived with us full-time for years, he still couldn't figure out where the silverware went when emptying the dishwasher. (Now that I think about it, neither can my husband. Hmmm.) Too, that might just be a thing for all kids. But, when kids shuttle back and forth between two homes and, sometimes, different lifestyles, confusion is bound to be had.

Where the ex may allow the kid to treat her entire house as a trash bin, your home may be Architectural Digest in waiting. Or, it could also be the reverse, with you the slob and the ex, Mrs. Clean. Where bedtime is only a suggestion at the ex's, your husband has a strict in-bed-by-8:30 PM policy. The ex demands the kids neatly fold and put away their clothes every day but you could not care one iota where their clothes go, including the floor. Because kids must live in alternate universes following a divorce and because there are a lot of rules kids have to learn just in one house, guess what? They're going to forget that drinking cereal milk from the bowl is verboten in your house despite mom's new spouse believing this gives the children the fine points on dining.

So, if you're a neat freak, give the stepkiddies a break when finding their clothes on the floor of the garage instead of in their closet. Or, if you live with fewer restrictions, don't be surprised if the stepkid is on *your* back to make your bed, do the dishes and clean up the joint. Kids don't do what they do with the sole aim of pissing you off. They do things because 1) Their little brains aren't fully formed, and they don't know what the hell they're doing half the time and 2) Who can keep up with rules from two houses?

Don't be disappointed if the kid doesn't remember you on Mother's Day.

This is a curious subject and one that evokes a lot of online chatter from stepmoms. On the one hand, you aren't "mom." On the other hand, you may do half the heavy lifting in child rearing, unless, of course, you are a self-centered jerk, leaving the kids exclusively to your husband, in which case, this doesn't apply to you. (Did you notice? No judgment here. Well, maybe a touch.) But, if you pack special lunches just for your stepkid, tell tall tales about pirates and treasures during bath time, help with homework, make costumes, kiss boo-boos and make them all better, change diapers … need I go on? … and Mother's Day arrives and there is nothing but crickets in the mailbox, a single ding of a text and nay a pot of roses on your doorstep, I ain't gonna' lie. It's gonna' suck. Big time.

Intellectually, you know you aren't "mom" to your stepkid and don't expect the same attention on Mother's Day as the kid gives to their mom. However, when emotions enter the arena, especially if bio-mom won't be receiving the Mother-of-the-Year award anytime soon, intellect says *adios* and now you're just plain pissed off. You swear to never lift another finger for that ungrateful kid again and will certainly not take them shopping next Mother's Day to buy their mom something wonderful when that chick won't return the favor for your husband on Father's Day. I mean, why should she receive a sappy card about what a wonderful mother she is? What about *your* Hallmark moment?

As we fast approach the end of this journey together, do I need to keep reminding you there are things you need not get excited or angry about? If you're still fuming from last Mother's Day and well-wishes were not yours, then allow me to remind you again: **Let it go!** *Feeling* like a mom doesn't make you *mom*.

Their not sending you a Mother's Day card doesn't necessarily mean they aren't fond of you, don't love you or that they don't consider you part of their family. You must consider all the dynamics that impact the kid and the mental aerobics they may go through on holidays like Mother's or Father's Day when their parents remarry. If tension between parents and significant others is a recurring theme, anything a kid might want to do for you on Mother's Day, even if making a card from construction paper, they may feel disloyal to their mom or suffer her wrath if she really hates your guts.

What's the safest position? Do nothing. Expect nothing.

For you, don't take it out on the kid, regardless of their age. For most mothers, their goal in having children wasn't to share her children's love and affection with a stranger. Yet, there you are, seemingly stealing some of mom's spotlight (and love and affection) on her special day. So, this is one day you have the ability to cut everyone a break. After all, it's not called *Step*mother's Day.

My Final Thoughts (And I'm Worn Out)

A s the 1968 Phillip Morris TV commercial for cigarettes cried: "You've come a long way, baby." (Got to love the 60s.)

I really do hope this book helps you along your stepmotherhood path. Being a stepmom can be a pretty thankless job and a job it is. You cook, clean, shop, plan and do two billion other things for people who may not even want you there. On the periphery, are one or more groups of people – a.k.a., in-laws, relatives of stepkids – who wouldn't shed a tear if they saw in the news that you went missing. Conversely, because I am nothing if not completely balanced in my views (I write this tongue in cheek so no need to send me hate email), there are some stepfamilies that somehow manage to stabilize and thrive. That should be our aim.

If, as you proclaim, you really do have your stepkid's best interest at heart, then you won't purposefully antagonize the kid's mother to where she feels the need to get you. And, if you've been sleeping through this book, allow me to remind you of why you took money from your bank and gave it to me for this book, which by the way, thank you, as I just found an amazing pair of mustard yellow shoes that would look amazing on me. Sorry, back to the point of this book. That is, and it is so incredibly simple and repeated ad nauseum throughout this book – kind of like beating you over the head until it sinks in – that you'll be the fool if you ignore my very sage wisdom: **STAY OUT OF THINGS**. Be nice. Be polite. Be invisible. Not to your husband, of course, as I showed you exactly where and when you need to share your thoughts with him, but to the few or many others who may be gunning for you.

Let the kid's parents sort out their relationship and if there are problems in that relationship, they are *their* problems. Not yours, unless the ex or others needlessly drag you into their fight, in which case, you still have a choice, girlfriend, as you can ignore it. I mean, you can't ignore a court summons, of course, but if you're invisible, a process server can't find you. Picture me shaking my head in complete confidence.

As I promised from the beginning, this book is not your typical kumbaya, blended family, let's-all-love-and-respect-each-other ... shall we say (I'm trying to refrain from swearing here), *bullshit*. Sorry. I just couldn't find a more appropriate word and go figure as I have the entire Internet at my disposal. Nope, this book was written exclusively to arm you with the knowledge and support you need to keep nutjobs at bay, a big ole' wad o' cash-ola in your pocket and to keep that hunka-hunka hubby of yours over the moon crazy about you. Anything complicated about this?

I'm harsh and to the point and it's what most people love about me. (I also exaggerate.) Everyone who knows me knows what I think about stuff. Being part of a stepfamily is no picnic at times. But why would anyone expect being part of a stepfamily to be different, considering that often times our *biological* family has more dysfunction than an entire season of Dr. Phil?

You see? I've got you all the way, girl.

As I was writing this epilogue, I thought how great it would be if I knew this book saved you a pile of cash, transformed your marriage and shut down the craziness in your head every time the ex and others conspired to run you out of town. I also thought it would be awesome to hear from those who hate my book and think I am full of it. And then it dawned on me! You can. Just email me: kathy@kathyhammondbooks.com

And need I say how much I would appreciate you leaving a review on Amazon ... or, on your blog or any other site where you wish to express your feelings – good or bad; though, hopefully, more good than bad. Unless, of course, you're a lawyer and then you'll probably want to send me a letter telling me how off-base I am even though you and I (and, now, a whole lot of readers) know the truth.

Now, stepmoms, go get 'em. Nothin' and no one can pull a fast one on you ever again. My work is done here. 😊

Made in the USA
Columbia, SC
09 August 2019